WHAT LEADEF ABOUT

THE WINNING QUALITIES OF HIGH IMPACT LEADERS

Dr. James O. Davis has devoted his life to working with high impact leaders in nearly every nation. When you read his latest book, *The Winning Qualities of High Impact Leaders,* you will learn firsthand what it takes to maximize and multiply your leadership even in the midst of life's greatest challenges. I believe every leader and their team should read this book!

—**Rev. Doug Clay**
General Superintendent
The General Council of the Assemblies of God
Springfield, Missouri

Dr. James O. Davis knows leadership, has spent countless hours with some of the greatest leaders in the world, and is eminently qualified to write this book, *The Winning Qualities of High Impact Leaders.* I don't know of any other person who can make a valid attempt at this book and pull it off.

Over the years, I have been in 23 nations with Dr. Davis; and on most occasions he has introduced me to the most influential church leader in every place. James knows leadership; but most importantly, they know him and fellowship with him and share their vision with him. That alone qualifies Dr. Davis to write this book.

But let's go a step further. Why would the greatest church leaders in the world become friends with Dr. Davis? The answer is simple, and the answer is the reason why you should read this book. Great leaders are motivated by great vision, and he has a great vision of carrying out the Great Commission by the year 2030.

— **Dr. Elmer Towns**
Cofounder, Liberty University
Lynchburg, Virginia

In *The Winning Qualities of High Impact Leaders,* Dr. James O. Davis has provided the quintessential guide to forming and fashioning the Christlike character required to build lasting influence that edifies your colleagues, enlarges your circle, and exalts your Lord. Get your copy today!

— **Dr. Sam Chand**
Sam Chand Leadership
Greater Atlanta, Georgia

"Each age . . . must write its own books," Ralph Waldo Emerson told Harvard College in his famous 1837 "The American Scholar" speech. This is *the* book for our age on Paul's command to "Run to Win!" (1 Corinthians 9:24), propelling us into the future with the ageless, ancient wisdom of Nehemiah. If you're only as good as your last book, Dr. James O. Davis just keeps getting better and better. I don't know how much better this book could have been.

— **Dr. Leonard Sweet**
Professor (Drew, George Fox, Tabor, Evangelical)
Founder/Chief contributor to preachthestory.com
Eastbound, Washington

When Dr. James O. Davis writes about high impact leaders, he is writing about himself. He displays the humility described in the Introduction and so would not consider himself as I just identified him. But it's true—he lives out the lessons of this book drawn from the life of Nehemiah. Every leader and every person who wants to lead must read this book. Dr. Davis models the principles he describes in this book.

—**Dr. Doug Beacham**
General Superintendent
International Pentecostal Holiness Church
Oklahoma City, Oklahoma

In *The Winning Qualities of High Impact Leaders,* Dr. James O. Davis has carefully articulated the personal leadership lessons to help you to build the walls of work, wisdom, wealth, and worship. Every wise master builder will greatly benefit from this powerful book!

—**Dr. Glenn Burris**
President
Foursquare Church
Los Angeles, California

Sooner or later, every visionary leader will face overwhelming odds to accomplish God's will for their lives. Dr. James O. Davis, in latest book, *The Winning Qualities of High Impact Leaders*, leads us through an intensive leadership study of the book of Nehemiah to show us the path to overcome the inward and outward struggles that keep us from spiritual success in this generation. If you're looking for a book on leadership, this will be a great tool for yourself and your entire team.

—**Dr. Carla Sunberg**
General Superintendent
Church of the Nazarene

In *The Winning Qualities of High Impact Leaders,* Dr. James O. Davis has provided the quintessential guide to designing your blueprint for a successful journey in life, family, and work. Dr. Davis has worked and served with high impact leaders throughout the world and is one of the most network leaders of this generation. I encourage you and your team to read this book!

— Dr. James Merritt
Founder
Cross Point Church
Touching Lives
Greater Atlanta, Georgia

In *The Winning Qualities of High Impact Leaders,* Dr. James O. Davis inspires us to choose the path and pace of our lives along with bringing together the best pacesetters to encourage us to get to the finish line. You will learn powerful wisdom lessons that will save you time, money, and energy on your journey to significance. Read it and reap from it!

— Rev. Peter Mortlock
Founder
City Impact Church
Auckland, New Zealand

Wow! What a book! I read *The Winning Qualities Of High Impact Leaders* in one sitting (that's how captivating the book is!) — and found it a treasure trove of compelling illustrations, pithy quotes, vital leadership principles, solid biblical insights, and great homespun wisdom! Dr. James O. Davis is a masterful storyteller, a competent exegete, and an insightful leader. A rare combination indeed! What I like most about this succinct book is that it doesn't just tell us "how to be a successful leader"; rather, it also redefines success for high impact leaders! I heartily recommend this excellent volume and intend to make it one of the key readings in my mentoring of leaders!

— Rev. Edmund Chan
Leadership Mentor, Covenant EFC
Founder, Global Alliance of Intentional
Disciplemaking Churches
Singapore

Dr. James O. Davis has devoted his life to working with high impact leaders in nearly every nation. He has been missional to interconnect every major Christian organization toward the fulfillment of the Great Commission in our time. When you read his latest book, *The Winning Qualities of High Impact Leaders*, based upon the Book of Nehemiah, you will learn how to cultivate and create powerful lifestyle principles of personal and professional victory. Get your copy today!

— Dr. David Uth
First Baptist of Orlando
Orlando, Florida

In *The Winning Qualities of High Impact Leaders,* Dr. James O. Davis, explains the strategy for success, the cures for discouragement, and the answers for anxiety. Dr. Davis goes on to describe and define what it takes to build the walls of dynamic leadership and live in personal revival throughout your life. I recommend this powerful book to you!

— **Dr. James Hudson Taylor IV**
President
China Evangelical Seminary
Taipei, Taiwan

Dr. James O. Davis and I have been friends for more than 25 years and have been fortunate to travel the world together. In his latest book, *The Winning Qualities of High Impact Leaders,* he challenges us like never before to develop and cultivate a winning, Christlike mindset to impact every sphere of our society today. When you read this book, you will learn how to fight ridicule, overcome fear, defeat demonic influences, break strongholds, and live in renewal and revival. I encourage you to buy enough books for your entire team!

— **Dr. David Sobrepena**
Founder
Word of Hope Church
Manilla, Philippines

You have been called by the Lord to be an overcomer! When you read Dr. James O. Davis's latest book, *The Winning Qualities of High Impact Leaders*, your faith will be challenged, your character will be enriched, and your mindset will be stretched to achieve more in the years ahead. This book is a must for all who wish to build the successful walls of wisdom, work, wealth, and worship in their lives.

— Rev. Randy Gilbert
Founder
Faith Landmarks Ministries
Richmond, Virginia

Dr. James O. Davis has mastered the art of discovering and then articulating life-altering biblical insights. In the 30 years I've known and called him friend, I've watched him model the qualities he discusses in this latest book. With a mix of memorable anecdotes, homiletic intentionality, impeccable interpretation, and spot-on application, *The Winning Qualities of High Impact Leaders* will serve well those godly people courageously trying to embody Jesus' character in the market place as well as church leaders laboring to make an eternal contribution with their lives.

— Dr. Terry Yancey
Assemblies of God Kansas Ministry Network
Maize, Kansas

Thank God for this brand-new piece from Dr. James O. Davis, *The Winning Qualities of High Impact Leaders*. He has always come with a bang to help other leaders in various ways. The Bible says that "iron sharpens iron, so one man sharpens another" (Proverbs 27:17). One of the best ways a leader can be better in leadership is not only to work with high impact leaders but also to read about them. This book affords the reader the opportunity to read at a glance the salient qualities of high impact leaders and apply them in order to make tremendous impact in contemporary leadership. I strongly recommend this book to many leaders who believe that their best is yet to come.

— Samson O. A. Ayokunle, Ph.D.
President, Christian Association of Nigeria &
Nigerian Baptist Convention

Dr. James O. Davis has devoted his life to working with high impact leaders in nearly every nation. I personally have been impacted by his courageous leadership to reach beyond my imagination. When you read his latest book, *The Winning Qualities of High Impact Leaders*, you will learn firsthand what it takes to maximize and multiply your leadership even during life's greatest challenges. I believe every leader and their team should read this book!

— Dr. Jo Anne Lyon
Ambassador
General Superintendent Emerita
The Wesleyan Church
Fishers, Indiana

Our Lord has not called us to become a people who sees difficulty in every opportunity but to become a people who sees opportunity but in every difficulty. Nehemiah was a royal cupbearer in the Persian court. He succeeded in using his favored position to have himself named governor of Judah. He is an outstanding example of godly leadership. In *The Winning Qualities of High Impact Leaders,* Dr. James O. Davis, giving fresh and inspiring insights from the life of Nehemiah, shows us how to learn from our past and at the same time lean into the future. Over the years, I have watched him synergize with the finest leaders for enormous outcomes. I encourage you to read his latest book and become a life-transformational leader!

—**Rev. Lazarus Yeghnazar**
Founder
222 Ministries
London, England

If you could go to singular source to learn the qualities of true, God-given success, would you take advantage of this opportunity? Of course, you would! In *The Winning Qualities of High Impact Leaders*, Dr. James O. Davis discusses what it takes to move from an influence leader to an impact leader. Over the last thirty-plus years, Dr. Davis has pulled together thousands of key leaders throughout world and has learned what it takes to build and rebuild and multiply and maximize for compounding results. I encourage you to get your copy of this book today!

—**Rev. Edgar Holder**
Living Stone Ministries
Rotterdam, Holland

In *The Winning Qualities of High Impact Leaders,* Dr. James O. Davis utilizes the ancient wisdom from the book Nehemiah to equip us for the modern age. These principles in Nehemiah will be true in the building of our mindset, our family, our business, our organization, and our lives. You will learn what it takes to be a winner in wisdom, work, wealth, and worship!

—**Rev. Stanley Hofwijks**
Maranatha Ministries
Amsterdam, Holland

I have had the privilege of working closely and traveling with Dr. James O. Davis. He is a leader among leaders and knows how to win and impact people and the world. His unique approach of examining the life of Nehemiah presents winning concepts that every leader needs to create winning strategies. *The Winning Qualities of High Impact Leaders* will challenge your thinking and transform your ministry and work.

—**Rev. Ejaz Nabie**
Faith Assembly
Richmond Hill, New York

Nehemiah's leadership was not that he acquired prestigious positions or that he was favored by his king. What he wanted more than anything was to use all this for God and for the people. He was not interested in building an impressive CV but in using his CV to lead the people back to God.

James O. Davis is a master of networking and leader cultivation. Some people may see James's global network of leaders as his greatest achievement; but like Nehemiah's CV was not his final goal, neither is this James's. From my conversations with James, his final goal is to provide every last person with the Word and he has reached out to key leaders to do this together. Through this, James accumulated huge experience and data on what makes a winning leader. His book, *The Winning Qualities of High Impact Leaders*, is the essence of what James has found to be the qualities of a great leader, not by our standards but God's. This book will take readers through the biblical definition of leaders as well as providing a comprehensive guide to what leaders in the twenty-first century must know. It is a privilege to be able to read in the comforts of our homes what James had to acquire through endless hours of travel; fellowship; and, of course, jetlag.

—Dr. Byoungho Zoh
Best-selling author of 50 books
Founder
Bible Tongdokwon
Seoul, Korea

The Winning Qualities of High Impact Leaders

Copyright © 2020 by James O. Davis

ISBN: 978-0-9908371-7-6

Billion Soul Publishing
Orlando, Florida
www.billionsoulpub.com

FOREWORD BY TOMMY BARNETT

THE
WINNING
QUALITIES
OF
HIGH IMPACT LEADERS

JAMES O. DAVIS
AFTERWORD BY TIMOTHY HILL

BILLION SOUL PUBLISHING

Orlando, Florida

DEDICATED TO

Evan O. Paul
A Devoted Husband, a Dedicated Father,
a Delightful Grandfather, a Dependable Friend,
and a Disciplined Christian

Your life inspires us to go farther!

CONTENTS

FOREWORD

In Vienna, Austria, Eliud Kipchoge of Kenya achieved a milestone once believed to be unattainable. On a misty Saturday morning on a course specially chosen for speed in an athletic spectacle of historic proportions, he ran 26.2 miles in a once inconceivable time of 1 hour 59 minutes 40 seconds!

In becoming the first person to cover the marathon distance in less than two hours, Kipchoge, 34, achieved a sports milestone and was granted almost mythical status in the running world by breaking through a temporal barrier that many would have deemed untouchable only a few years ago.

Kipchoge, an eight-time major marathon winner and three-time Olympic medalist, pounded his chest twice as he crossed the finish line in Vienna's leafy Prater Park where the majority of the run had unfolded on a long straightaway of recently paved road with roundabouts on either end.

For Kipchoge, the feat merely burnished his credentials as the world's greatest marathoner. "Together, when we run, we can make this world a beautiful world," Kipchoge said after finishing.

I am quite sure, along life's journey, there had been more times than we will ever know that he did not want to practice and no doubt numerous times during a race when he wanted to quit. Yet he was not a "no show" on race day! What he began, he saw to the finish. His final words, "Together, when we run, we can make this world a beautiful world," challenge us to run our Christian race to the finish line.

There will be times when we don't want to show up for our practice sessions in prayer and Bible study. While we are running to overcome life's challenges, there will be instances when we wonder if it is all worth it or will feel like giving up, giving in, and giving over to the temptations of the world.

When Kipchoge broke the 2-hour marathon, he had 41 pacesetters who helped to keep a world record pace. In other words, he chose to surround himself with champions who believed it was possible to break a 2-hour marathon. A pacesetter, sometimes informally called a rabbit, is a runner who leads a middle- or long-distance running event to ensure a fast time and avoid excessive tactical racing. Pacesetters serve the role of conveying tangible information about pacing on the track during a race.

In *The Winning Qualities of High Impact Leaders*, you will not only learn what it takes to win in work, wisdom, wealth, and worship but will also know the kinds of pacesetters you will want to have around you to help you to run successfully to the finish line. Here is an amazing reality: While you choose the path and the pace of your life, you can also pull together powerful pacesetters who will encourage you to keep on keeping on throughout the decades of your journey.

I have been fortunate to be one of the pastors of one of the five largest churches in the USA and to have had the opportunity to go to Los Angeles and open the Dream Center. I learned many years ago that you have to grow by addition, not subtraction. You can only be stronger by adding on more than refusing to take on anything else.

For example, I realized I had a lot of wasted time: waiting for appointments, planes, etc. If I could use that wasted time, I would be able to accomplish more things than I wanted. All of 12 my books were written during wasted time. I've found that it is an awesome point of time that you can change people's lives and relationships and do the business the way you need it to be done. The biggest thing it helps me do is accomplish my dreams. Too many people have dreams they will never accomplish but could if they would learn to make the disciplined decisions necessary for success.

The Dream Center is a dream that I personally had for 40 years. I realized that I was turning 60 years of age and had previously had a dream of running across America. I decided to run across the Mojave Desert to raise the funds needed to open the Dream Center. It took me 19 days — the equivalent of running a marathon per day. We were able to raise the amount we needed to make the down payment on the building that is now the Dream Center!

I would have never been able to lead great soul-winning churches, launch and build the Dream Center (nearly 300 Dream Centers today), travel, and preach throughout the world if I had not had learned what it truly takes to win in life and the kinds of encouraging pacesetters needed to help me to get across the finish line.

If we run together, we can do more than make this world a "beautiful world"; we can make it a saved world.

Dr. James Davis is truly a world changer. He has traveled the world in search of fellow pacesetters who are racing to the finish line to carry out the Great Commission.

Pastor Tommy Barnett
Founder
The Dream City Church
Phoenix, Arizona
The Dream Center
Los Angeles, California

ACKNOWLEDGMENTS

If this book deserves and delights a wide readership,
it is because of Michele Buckingham and Jackie Chrisner.
These two editors took my transcripts and articles and
turned them into a coherent whole. I am grateful
for their friendship and partnership!

THE WINNING QUALITIES OF HIGH IMPACT LEADERS

Building the Walls of Work, Wisdom, Wealth, and Worship

INTRODUCTION

How does you measure a winning leader? What is the essence of "true winning" in this life? What are the qualities of winning leadership? What are the inner strengths that compel leaders to overcome the inevitable obstacles that will come their way? Many years ago, Dr. Dennis Waitley stated, "You can always spot the losers in life. The losers in life spend the majority of their time making others look bad so they can look good" (*The Psychology of Winning*, Berkley, New York, 1986, audio). In other words, I do not have to become a bigger person if I can make you look smaller in the eyes of people. How do we measure ourselves?

Nearly two thousand years ago, the Apostle Paul was revisiting a strategic mission field. He came to Miletus, and there he gathered with him the Ephesian elders. He took time to walk with them down memory lane. They talked about the good times they had together—how God had blessed and poured out His blessing. Paul rehearsed it all.

> *And when he had said these things, he knelt down and prayed with them all. Then they all wept freely, and fell on Paul's neck and kissed him, sorrowing most of all for the words which he spoke, that they would see his face no more. And they accompanied him to the ship* (Acts 20:36-38).

Use your imagination. They were one in the bonds of love. They had been through so many prayer meetings and evangelistic crusades together. They had had so many victories in Jesus. Their hearts were melded together, and now they were having a prayer meeting. They were all on their knees. God moved into that prayer meeting, and there was such a sweet spirit.

When you are gone, are you going to be missed?

As they were praying, they realized this was the last prayer meeting they would ever have with Paul the Apostle on earth. They began to weep…not just a few tears; they were convulsing. The Bible says, *they all wept freely* (Acts 20:37). Then they began to hug Paul's neck; they just fell on his neck. They were weeping and squeezing him and hugging him because they knew never again on this earth would they see Paul. Then they walked down to the wharf where the ship was. Paul got on that ship; and as it began to sail, they were standing there weeping because Paul was leaving, never to return.

When you are gone, are you going to be missed? I mean…other than by your family. Are you going to be missed? Will it make any difference? We are going either by rapture or by death, but we are all going. The question is: When you go, what difference will it make? Is your life going to have any kind of lasting impact?

I heard of a man who had surgery and woke up in the recovery room where all of the windows were covered by curtains and the blinds were drawn. He called to the nurse, "Nurse, open the windows; I want to see outside. Who closed the blinds anyway?" She said, "Just calm down. I closed them. There's a big fire across the street, and I didn't want you to wake up and think the operation was not a success."

Some of us are going to wake up and find that our life was not a success. We will go into eternity with a wasted life. When we go, we are going to leave behind all that we have and take all that we are.

When the world measures a leader, it measures them by brains, by brawn, or by bucks.

When the world measures a leader, it measures them by brains, by brawn, or by bucks. How do you measure a leader? Michael Letito is in the *Guinness Book of World Records*. Do you know what his claim to fame is? Eating glass and metal. He grinds it up and eats it. Mixes it in with his Wheaties or whatever he eats. Since 1966, he has eaten ten bicycles as well as eating a supermarket cart in four and a half days. He ate six chandeliers in addition to a Cessna light aircraft. Can you imagine this fellow reporting into Jesus: "My son, what did you do when you were on earth?" "Lord, I ate an airplane." What a claim to fame. What really counts? What really matters? How do you measure your life?

In *The Winning Qualities of High Impact Leaders*, you will find the guts required for glory and the walk required for winning. With these introductory thoughts, I strive to set the stage to compel you to go farther than you ever believed possible in your life. We need to stretch for success.

The Manner of the Winning Leader

We measure a leader by the manner of their life. *From Miletus he sent to Ephesus and called for the elders of the church.*

And when they had come to him, he said to them: "You know,
from the first day that I came to Asia, in what manner I always
lived among you, serving the Lord with all humility, with many
tears and trials which happened to me by the plotting of the Jews
(Acts 20:17-19).

What was the manner of Paul's life? His life was a life
of **humility**. *Serving the Lord with all humility*. I believe with
all my heart that no one has a life worth living, no one
has a life that can be called a great life for there is no true
greatness without true humility. Humility is not putting
yourself down. It is not saying you are no good because
that is not true about you.

When God measures a leader's life,
he does not measure the leader's life by how
many servants the leader has but by how
many men the leader serves.

Do not get the idea that humility is not loving yourself.
The Bible says we are to love others as we love ourselves.
If you do not love yourself, I am afraid of you because
you do not know how to love me.

What is humility? An honest estimation of yourself that
says about you what God says about you, and it results
primarily in serving. Notice in that verse he says, *serving*
the Lord with all humility. The word "serving" is the verb
form of the noun "doulos" which means "bond slave." Do
you know what the mark of humility is? Serving others. A
humble person is a person who serves other people.

When God measures a leader's life, he does not
measure the leader's life by how many servants the leader
has but by how many men the leader serves. There are
a lot of people whose lives are going to amount to little

more than a zero with the edges trimmed off because they have never learned to serve. Unless you are a servant, you are not going to be truly missed when you are gone.

Not only is there a life of humility, but there is also a life of **heartache**. Paul says, *serving the lord with all humility, with many tears*. The Apostle Paul had a broken heart. He knew how to weep and how to enter into the sorrows and hurts of other people. That is the way to be missed.

If you live for self and self alone and try to insulate yourself from the cares and toils and problems of this world, you are not going to be missed. We need to be a person who knows how to sympathize, a person who knows how to empathize, a person who has the compassion of the Lord Jesus in our heart and life.

The Apostle Paul said, "I serve the Lord with humility. I serve the Lord with heartache." And then he says, "I serve the Lord with **hardship**." He speaks in verse 19 of the many trials that befell him. Paul faced and fought many trials. It literally means that there were people who disliked him, people who opposed him, people who harmed him physically because of the stand he took for the Lord Jesus Christ.

There is no way, absolutely no way, that you can have a life that will count and make an impression on this world without making some enemies. We will learn a lot about our enemies in this book. As we embark on the task of rebuilding the walls of our lives or reviving a discouraged people, satanic enemies will try to stop us from achieving great outcomes for the glory of God.

You may say, "I don't want that kind of a life." Well, maybe you don't. Maybe you just want to be all wrapped up in yourself; but when you are gone, it is not going to make much difference. Nobody in this world will say, "That's the way to have a winning life."

The Message of a Winning Leader

Not only do we live a certain way, but we also say a certain thing. We are going to leave behind a message. Every one of us will be known for something when we are gone. They will think about us. Do you know what I want them to think about when they think about me? The gospel of Christ. I want them to say, "That man's life was centered in the only message that really matters." Paul says, *I kept back nothing that was helpful, but proclaimed it to you, and taught you publicly and from house to house* (that is, in every place), *testifying to Jews, and also to Greeks* (every person), *repentance toward God and faith toward our Lord Jesus Christ* (Acts 20:20-21 Emphasis added).

That was the **content** of his message, that which encapsulated his life: repentance and faith — repentance toward God and faith toward our Lord Jesus Christ. Paul was known primarily as a gospel preacher. It was a narrow message, and he kept on preaching that message.

Notice the **conviction** of it. *And see, now I go bound in the spirit to Jerusalem, not knowing the things that will happen to me there, except that the Holy Spirit testifies in every city, saying that chains and tribulations await me* (Acts 20:22-23). Paul is saying, "I'm going back to Jerusalem. The Spirit of God wants me to go. I'm bound in the Spirit." That is, he knew it was God's will for him to go; and when he got there, he knew he was going to have heartache and trouble.

Paul then says, *But none of these things move me; nor do I count my life dear to myself, so that I may finish my race with joy, and the ministry which I received from the Lord Jesus, to testify to the gospel of the grace of God* (Acts 20:24).

You want a life that counts? You are going to have to have a message that has the right content and the right conviction. Paul said, *I go bound in the spirit* and *none of these things move me*. Nothing was going to stop him.

Paul had a bulldog grip on certain things. Are you that way? Do you know what is wrong with the average leader? They have opinions, not convictions. Paul said, "I am bound in the Spirit. I am going to finish my course with joy. I will do it." Then he said, "I know what I'm going to," and it eventually led to his death. However, Paul would rather die with a conviction than live with a compromise. How about you? I stand amazed at how many Christian leaders are more concerned about their "brand" than making Jesus known throughout the earth without caring who gets the credit. When they are gone, they will not be missed.

Do you know what is wrong with the average leader? They have opinions, not convictions.

Most of us had far rather live with compromise than to die with conviction. You can understand why Paul was the man that he was, and how this shames me as I think of the content of his message.

We also need to understand the **confidence** of his message. Paul died confidently. *And indeed, now I know that you all, among whom I have gone preaching the kingdom of God, will see my face no more. Therefore I testify to you this day that I am innocent of the blood of all men. For I have not shunned to declare to you the whole counsel of God* (Acts 20:25-27).

Wow! Did you hear that? Paul said, "You're not going to see me anymore. I'm going on to heaven; but I'm going to tell you one thing: I'm pure from the blood of all men."

He was moved for the souls of men; he was talking about soul winning. Do you have a soul goal? If we do not tell our friends, our neighbors, our brothers, our sisters about the Lord Jesus Christ and they die and go to hell, their blood is on our hands.

The Apostle Paul knew that before long he was going to have to meet the Lord, and he said, "I am pure. I am free from the blood of all men. I am not going to face my Lord with bloody hands." I know many men who know their favorite team's stats but do not know the names of the lost souls who live next door to them. They are going to face the Lord with blood on their hands.

Every person has a motto for their life. Maybe they have put it into words; maybe they have not.

I see the Apostle Paul. He is in his cell…tired and aware that his execution is to come. The burley guard comes to the cell door. "Paul, come!" "Where are we going?" "You're going to the chopping block, Paul. We're going to execute you." And he comes with a chain to bind Paul who says, "You don't need to put that chain on me. I can walk. It's alright. Don't worry. Let's go." And so the guard takes Paul, and they begin to walk down toward the Tiber River, the river that will soon drink the blood of the great apostle.

There he goes, the greatest Christian who ever lived. Can you see the little humpbacked Jew with his little gray head and squinty eyes hobbling along with his body bent, broken, and scarred from the whippings, the stonings, the imprisonments, as well as from being pickled in the Mediterranean Sea?

The guard says, "Do I hear music? Are you humming?" Paul says, "Oh yeah, I didn't know you were listening to me. Just a little song that we love to sing: 'It will be worth it all when we see Jesus.'" The guard says, "You're a… you're a strange one." When they arrive at the river, the executioner says, "Tie him to the chopping block." Paul responds, "You don't need to tie me. It's all right." And he kneels down and puts his neck on the chopping block.

The guard says, "Aren't you afraid, Paul?" "Oh," he says, "I've done this before." "You can't have." "Oh, I die daily." And so they put his head on the chopping block. "Any last words, Paul?" "Oh yes, I'm glad you asked. Here are my last words: Jesus Christ is Lord! Jesus died and was risen for you!" And the ax falls, and the head falls into the basket.

The next scene is heaven. Paul is looking into the face of the King of the Universe, Jesus Christ. "Lord Jesus, you know I was not strong, I was not handsome, I did not have a good voice, I did not have much money; but Lord, I kept the faith. I finished my job. Lord, I fought a good fight. The race is over. Lord, these hands are pure from the blood of all men." How would you like to meet the Lord like that? I believe the Lord Jesus said to him, "Well done, good and faithful servant. Enter into the joy of the Lord. Thank you, Paul, for being true to me." Many men and women are going to meet the Lord with bloody hands. They may make heaven; but they will hold in their bloody hands the ashes of a wasted life!

The Motto of the Winning Leader

We then measure a leader by the **motto** of their life. Every person has a motto for their life. Maybe they have put it into words; maybe they have not. However, there is something that impels them, something that motivates them, something that drives them, something that constrains them. Paul's constraint was, *I have coveted no one's silver or gold or apparel. Yes, you yourselves know that these hands have provided for my necessities, and for those who were with me. I have shown you in every way, by laboring like this, that you must support the weak. And remember the words* *of the Lord Jesus, that He said, "It is more blessed to give than to receive"* (Acts 20:33-35).

The Apostle Paul was a great leader because he spent life not primarily as a receiver but as a giver; therefore, his life was blessed.

Life is divided into two categories: the takers and the givers. The takers eat better; the givers sleep better. When you die, all you are going to take with you is what you have given away. What you have spent is gone forever and what you did not spend will be left for others, but what you gave away is yours forever. It is more blessed to give than to receive.

I want you to see what that motto did for Paul. It freed him from covetousness. His testimony was, *I have coveted no one's silver or gold or apparel* (v. 33). His philosophy also freed him from idleness (v. 34). Paul held up his hands and said, "I have ministered unto my necessities. I worked for my needs."

Paul said there are people who are weak, people who cannot work, people who have needs; but he worked so that he might help the needy. The Bible says that if a man will not work, neither should he eat; but there are some people who cannot work, and those of us who can work need to work to help those who are weak.

What was the motto of Paul's life? *It is more blessed to give than to receive* (v. 35). It saved him from covetousness. It saved him from idleness. It saved him from selfishness. Nobody has a winning life that lives a selfish life. The Apostle Paul lived a life of giving, not taking; of helping, not hurting; of loving and lifting and caring.

I encourage you to let this story move you and challenge you to evaluate the essence of who you are in this life. Remember: It is more blessed to give than to receive.

During World War II, the Nazis came into a Polish village and accused all of the Jews in that village of crimes against the State. They brought them out of their houses to a particular field and made them dig a ditch that would later become their grave. They then stripped them of their clothes, lined those Polish Jews up against a wall, took their machine guns, and began to mow them down. The people fell like cordwood, head over heels into the grave.

A little ten-year-old boy was standing there naked with his mother and daddy. The bullets ripped their bodies open, and the blood splattered everywhere. As they fell, the little boy fell with them also; but he was not touched by one bullet. He fell in the grave and lay still. The Nazis assumed he was dead because he was splattered with blood. They began to push the dirt over these people and buried that little ten-year-old boy alive. However, his face was in such a position that he caught a pocket of air where the ground was not packed so hard. He could actually breathe under the ground, lying on the mutilated bodies of his loved ones. After several hours when it was dark, he began to dig out of his own grave and clawed his way to the surface.

He was naked and covered with blood and dirt. He went to the house of a neighbor and knocked on the door. When the woman opened the door and saw that little boy covered with blood and dirt and caked with the remains of his grave, she recognized him as one of the Jewish boys and knew that he had been marked for death.

She screamed at him, "Go away!" and slammed the door in his face. The little boy dragged himself to another door and knocked on it and begged for help, and the same thing happened. The woman said with terror in her voice, "No, I cannot help you! Go away!" He went to a third door and knocked on the door. When the woman opened the door, she looked at him and her face froze; but before she could say anything, he said to her, "Don't you recognize me? I am the Jesus that you say you love." She broke and said, "Come in. Come in." At the risk of her own life, she sheltered that ten-year-old child. Jesus said, *Inasmuch as you did it to one of the least of these My brethren, you did it to Me* (Matthew 25:40).

There are millions of men and women who, when they are gone, will not be missed.

There is no easy way to be a winning leader. It is more blessed to give than it is to receive. There are millions of men and women who, when they are gone, will not be missed. However, there are others who, when they are gone, will be sorely wept over. These are the leaders who know the things that count. How do we measure a winning leader's life? By the manner of their life, the message of their life, and the motto of their life.

As I have pondered and prayed over *The Winning Qualities of a Visionary Leader*, I found myself saying at times, "I have a long way to go in this area or in that area." We never fully achieve everything we can truly become on this side of heaven. However, I believe if you read this book carefully, you will find inspiration and introspection, renewal and reflection, and values and victory.

1

—

THE WINNING MINDSET
TO OVERCOME

Sooner or later, all of us will face a setback in our vision
and mission in life. It is inevitable; yet it is what we do
with what comes our way that will determine whether or
not the setback becomes a comeback. When leaders face a
setback, they often panic. The word "panic" is taken from
the Greek word "to choke." To choke means to cut off, to
disengage, to disconnect. When you panic, you cut off the
air to your brain; when you cut off the air to your brain,
you cannot think clearly; and when you are unable to
think clearly, you are unable to make wise decisions.

I am not implying that you should develop a "happy-
go-lucky" attitude when a disastrous setback comes your
way. There has be a balance between the happy-by-and-by
and the nasty-now-and-now. History is replete with
multiple examples of people who panicked and made
poor decisions. During the stock market crash of 1929,
thousands of people panicked and committed suicide; but
the market came back, bigger and better than before! That
stock market crash was called a crisis.

"Crisis" is a word with dual meanings: great challenge
and/or great opportunity! In the landmark book, *Think
and Grow Rich*, Napoleon Hill states, "In every adver-
sity there is always the seed for equal or greater benefit"

(The Ralston Society, 1937). We must learn that tough times do not last, but tough people do. We cannot panic but must be committed to working on our goals and personal achievement all the time. There is an expression in the real estate world: "The time to buy is when there's blood in the streets" (Baron Rothschild). In other words, when it is very bad and desperate, be the contrarian, the optimist, and do something positive in a most negative situation.

"Crisis" is a word with dual meanings: great challenge and/or great opportunity!

Nehemiah lived in desperate times. He was not able to choose the time in which he would live, but he could choose how he would respond to what had happened to his people in the previous generation. He provides a powerful and personal example of a visionary who saw things before they were and had a plan to turn major setbacks into a masterful comeback!

The Jewish people had been in captivity in Babylon for 70 years. In 530 BC, the armies of Persia broke the Babylonian supremacy, and the king of Persia released the Jewish remnant, encouraging them to return to Jerusalem. At that time, 50,000 Israelites did return and immediately began to reconstruct the demolished temple. They soon became discouraged by opposition from the people who had settled there during the captivity and abandoned their task. Years later, Haggai and Zechariah appeared on the scene and challenged them to finish the job. They did this 20 years after their return.

Sixty more years passed; and under Ezra's leadership, more of the remnant returned to Jerusalem. Although the temple had been rebuilt, the walls of the city were in shambles and the gates burned; so for 90 years after the first Jews returned, the people of God lived in affliction and shame in a city with broken walls and burned gates. It was then that God prepared Nehemiah and called him into service during the rebuilding of the walls of Jerusalem. It was his task to leave the security of his home and be the agent of God in bringing revival to his people by rebuilding the walls. The walls represented salvation and the gates praise.

So I answered them, and said to them, "The God of heaven Himself will prosper us; therefore we His servants will arise and build, but you have no heritage or right or memorial in Jerusalem" (Nehemiah 2:20). Don't you like that verse? *The God of heaven Himself will prosper us; therefore we His servants will arise and build.*

Have you ever had any problems? Well, wonderful! Congratulations! A problem really is an opportunity in disguise. We need to learn that God wants us to see our problems as possibilities and our adversaries as opportunities. As Christians, we are not a people who sees difficulty in every opportunity; to the contrary, we are a people who sees opportunity in every difficulty.

We need to learn that God wants us to see our problems as possibilities and our adversaries as opportunities.

Whether we in our ministry are going to try to turn a problem into a possibility or whether you, as an individual, are transforming your problem into a possibility, we are going to see that God has a wonderful plan for us.

There are three paradigm shifts to getting ready to do anything great and glorious in the name of Jesus, three steps in achieving our maximum potential.

WE NEED TO VISUALIZE OUR CIRCUMSTANCES

The words of Nehemiah the son of Hachaliah. It came to pass in the month of Chislev, in the twentieth year, as I was in Shushan the citadel, that Hanani one of my brethren came with men from Judah; and I asked them concerning the Jews who had escaped, who had survived the captivity, and concerning Jerusalem. And they said to me, "The survivors who are left from the captivity in the province are there in great distress and reproach. The wall of Jerusalem is also broken down, and its gates are burned with fire" (Nehemiah 1:1-3).

At this time, Nehemiah is in Persia; and he has seen certain brethren who have recently been in Jerusalem. They had no television, no radio, no newspapers as we know them, no Internet, no cell phones; and yet Nehemiah wanted some news. He said, "What is the city of God like? I want to know. Tell it to me, so I can visualize it, so I can see it."

As they brought this report, I am certain they wept as they said, "Oh, Nehemiah, you cannot believe the degradation. You cannot believe the desolation. You cannot believe the danger. You cannot believe the depression. The city is in disarray. The gates have been burned with fire. The walls have crumbled. The streets are filled with weeds and trash and debris. The people are discouraged; the people are in poverty; the people are hungry."

Nehemiah saw a city with walls that had crumbled. We are going to learn that a large part of the Book of Nehemiah is the story of the rebuilding of these walls. These walls were literal walls in that day, but we are asking a question not only, "What did it mean then?" but also "What does it mean today?" because the walls are also symbolic. Walls stand for protection. Walls are symbolic of separation. Walls spoke of the glory of God. In the Bible, walls and especially those around the city of Jerusalem had a symbolic meaning. They spoke of the glory of God, the salvation of God, the protection of God over His people; and yet the walls had fallen.

What does this mean to us today? We are called to rebuild walls that are in decay. Please think for a moment about some walls that have fallen to the ground, some walls that are in disarray. We are told that nations decay and the walls of national defense usually fall into nine cycles. This is called the *Tytler Cycle in History*. Alexander Fraser Tytler (October 15, 1747-January 5, 1813) was a Scottish advocate, judge, writer, and historian who served as Professor of Universal History and Greek and Roman Antiquities at the University of Edinburgh. Following is his summary of democracy where people go from:

1. Bondage to spiritual faith.
2. Spiritual faith to courage.
3. Courage to liberty.
4. Liberty to abundance.
5. Abundance to selfishness.
6. Selfishness to complacency.
7. Complacency to apathy.
8. Apathy to dependence.
9. Dependence back again to bondage.

No matter where we live, it is time for us take our place along the walls and rebuild the walls of spiritual defense that God wants us to have for our respective nations.

Domestic Walls

In 1870, only 2-3 percent of the marriages in America ended in divorce. Today, over 39 percent of marriages end in divorce. I am grateful to report that the divorce rate has been gradually dropping since the 1980s.

What was horrible yesterday is acceptable today and has become a stepping-stone for something worse tomorrow.

There is a militant war being waged against the home. Many of the feminists today are anti-home. With these extreme liberal ideas, they strive to destroy the nuclear family and come after the children. They want society to raise children instead of parents. They want to take our children, teach our children, brainwash our children, and indoctrinate our children to the new society—the new way of doing things. Throughout the world, the family is the foundation of any nation. As go the families, so go the nations.

Decency Walls

The walls of decency are decaying. Look at what is happening to us. Pass the newsstand, and pornography will stare you in the face as if a broken sewer line were overflowing. We have ceased to be shocked. What used to amaze us now just simply amuses us. The sins that used to slink down back allies now parade down Main Street. What was horrible yesterday is acceptable today and has become a stepping-stone for something worse tomorrow.

Can a man take fire to his bosom, and his clothes not be burned? Can one walk on hot coals, and his feet not be seared? (Proverbs 6:27-28) Can a person feed on garbage and it not affect his health?

Look at the wall of decency in our educational system. What has happened to our educational system? Why are students running wild? Because we have taken prayer out of and expelled God from our schools; consequently, with the Bible and God out and evolution in, homosexuality, illicit sex, murderous abortion, and venereal disease are rampant.

I feel badly for the school teacher who stands up and tells kids, "You must do right," and they say, "Teacher, what is right and where do you get right from? Who says what is right and who says what is wrong unless there's a God in Heaven who does?" We must get back to the Word of God and the God of the Word. How can we morally govern anyone unless we come back to moral foundations? *If the foundations are destroyed, what can the righteous do?* (Psalm 11:3).

Doctrinal Walls

In addition to the walls of decency crumbling, the walls of doctrine have also fallen. There is not a lot wrong in any nation that could not be changed if we had a generation of preachers who would stand in the pulpit and preach, *Thus says the* LORD *of hosts* (Jeremiah 29:4). I believe that with all my heart. I believe church attendance is down because preaching is down.

We have many ministers who are preaching the gospel, and I thank God for them; but we have many who no longer believe that the Bible is the inerrant, infallible Word of God. Many times the congregation does not know that because they do not have enough courage to stand in front of people and say, "I no longer believe this book." They are taking their salary under false pretenses and should get out of the ministry.

Liberalism is a parasite. It has no power to build. It does not build orphanages or colleges or churches.

Liberalism is a parasite. It has no power to build. It does not build orphanages or colleges or churches. It is a parasite that crawls into institutions that have been built by Bible-believers. The walls of doctrine and theology have crumbled, and it is time that God's people started to rebuild them.

Of course, we are to love people as individuals — whoever they are, wherever they are, whatever their philosophy, whatever their creed, whatever their race, whatever their color — they are to be loved for Jesus Christ loves them. However, we are not to tolerate godless philosophies that are taking our country apart one brick at a time. The walls have fallen, and it is time that we open our eyes and see that the walls have fallen.

What motivated Nehemiah's heart, head, and hands was that he could visualize the situation. Take a few moments to see your city and nation for what is today. Once our hearts and minds have seen it, we will never be able to go back to where we were in our thinking of the past. Visionary leadership learns from the past and leans into the future! When Jesus saw "the city," He wept over it.

WE NEED TO AGONIZE OVER
OUR CONDITIONS

Nehemiah was a layman, not a priest like Ezra nor a prophet like Malachi. He served the Persian king in a secular position before leading a group of Jews to Jerusalem in order to rebuild the city walls. Nehemiah's expertise in the king's court adequately equipped him for the political and physical reconstruction necessary for the remnant to survive.

Under Nehemiah's leadership, the Jews withstood opposition and came together to accomplish their goal. Nehemiah led by example, giving up a respected position in a palace for hard labor in a politically insignificant district. He partnered with Ezra, who also appears in this book, to solidify the political and spiritual foundations of the people. Nehemiah's humility before God (see his moving intercessory prayers in Chapters 1 and 9) provided an example for the people. He did not claim glory for himself but always gave God the credit for his successes.

Nehemiah recorded the reconstruction of the wall of Jerusalem, Judah's capital city. Together, he and Ezra, who led the spiritual revival of the people, directed the political and religious restoration of the Jews in their homeland after the Babylonian captivity.

Nehemiah's life provides a fine study on leadership. He overcame opposition from outsiders as well as internal turmoil. He exercised his administrative skills in his strategy to use half the people for building while the other half kept watch for the Samaritans who, under Sanballat, threatened attack (Nehemiah 4-7). As governor, Nehemiah negotiated peace among the Jews who were unhappy with Persian taxes. He exhibited a steadfast determination to complete his goals. Accomplishing those goals resulted in a people encouraged, renewed, and excited about their future.

The second paradigm shift required to developing a winning mindset to overcome is to **agonize over our condition:** *So it was, when I heard these words, that I sat down and wept, and mourned for many days; I was fasting and praying before the God of heaven* (Nehemiah 1:4).

We Need a Prayer of Contrition

What kind of a prayer was this? It was a prayer of contrition. It was a prayer where Nehemiah wept salty tears over the condition as it was. Do you know what is wrong with our society? Our society has forgotten how to blush, and the church has forgotten how to weep.

Do you know what is wrong with our society? Our society has forgotten how to blush, and the church has forgotten how to weep.

When was the last time you spent a night in prayer? When was the last time you fasted and prayed? When was the last time you shed a tear over some soul that was mortgaged to the devil?

We often pray without crying, give without sacrifice, and live without fasting. Is it any wonder that we sow without reaping? Weeping, fasting, praying, and seeking the face of God have become a lost art. For revival to come to any nation or society, God's people need to begin to pray a prayer of contrition—a prayer of brokenness. This is the generation of a dry-eyed church in a hell-bent world.

Do not read over the words, *I sat down*, too quickly. He stopped everything he was doing and focused on the terrible news he just received. He sat down and contemplated the seemingly overwhelming context of the state of Jerusalem. We are often in such a hurry that we miss the weight of the moment or do not feel the intensity of the pain of a society that has gone down the wrong road against the Lord.

We Need a Prayer of Confession

Nehemiah's prayer not only contained contrition but also confession: *Please let Your ear be attentive and Your eyes open, that You may hear the prayer of Your servant which I pray before You now, day and night, for the children of Israel Your servants, and confess the sins of the children of Israel which we have sinned against You. Both my father's house and I have sinned* (Nehemiah 1:6).

The confession of his prayer was both national and personal. Nehemiah said, "Israel has sinned, and I have sinned." We must pray for our city, we must pray for our state, and we must pray for our nation. We must repent nationally; however, this is no good unless we repent individually.

Have you repented? We must do more than sit, weep, mourn, and bow our heads. We must repent. If we do not repent, we will never be a part of the solution—only part of the problem.

We Need a Prayer of Confidence

Nehemiah prayed a prayer of confidence: *Remember, I pray, the word that You commanded Your servant Moses, saying, "If you are unfaithful, I will scatter you among the nations; but if you return to Me, and keep My commandments and do them, though some of you were cast out to the farthest part of the heavens, yet I will gather them from there, and bring them to the place which I have chosen as a dwelling for My name" Now these are Your servants and Your people, whom You have redeemed by Your great power, and by Your strong hand* (Nehemiah 1:8-10).

Did you notice what he is doing? He is saying, "God, do you remember what you said in your Word? Do you remember those promises you made in your Word? God, I'm holding you to your Word." That is what real prayer is.

Real prayer is not just letting your mind wander and thinking up some things that you want and reaching out to heaven with a shopping list.

Real prayer is not just letting your mind wander and thinking up some things that you want and reaching out to heaven with a shopping list. Real prayer is rooted in the rock-ribbed promises of the Word of God. It is finding a promise in the Word of God and standing on it.

God says, *Concerning the work of My hands, you command Me* (Isaiah 45:11). Nehemiah audaciously came to the Father and said, "Father, I am praying a prayer of confidence. I am believing you, God, because you promised; and because you promised, Lord, I am holding you to your Word."

We serve a majestic God. Martin Luther, the Protestant reformer, stated that "Prayer is not overcoming God's reluctance, but laying hold of His willingness" (Goodreads.com/Martin Luther Quotes). Find a promise in the Word of God that means it is something God wants to do and then stand upon it and pray huge prayers.

John Newton said, "Thou art coming to a King, Large petitions with thee bring; For His grace and pow'r are such none can ever ask too much" (Goodreads.com/John Newton Quotes).

We Need a Prayer of Commitment

Nehemiah prays a prayer of commitment: *O LORD, I pray, please let Your ear be attentive to the prayer of Your servant, and to the prayer of Your servants who desire to fear Your name; and let Your servant prosper this day, I pray, and grant him mercy in the sight of this man. For I was the king's cupbearer* (Nehemiah 1:11).

Nehemiah had a very important job as the king's cupbearer. Here was a fantastically, lavishly wealthy king — so wealthy that he had a cupbearer who would come in with his wine and his goodies every day and offer them to him. This was a well-paying position as well as a highly elevated position because Nehemiah was right there with the king in his most intimate moments.

Nehemiah had a job of luxury. He was far removed from the poverty and the degradation and the fallen walls. Nehemiah was in his little place of security. He was in his own little warm nest.

"You can do more than pray after you have prayed, but you cannot do more than pray until you have prayed."

Yet he could not stay there as God had burdened him. When he saw the condition of the fallen walls, he said, "By the grace of God, I'm going to get involved. Lord, I'm starting to do something; I feel a fire burning in me. God, you're calling me now, and you will prosper me because

I am about to get out of my warm nest and commit to rebuild the walls."

It is not enough to pray a prayer of contrition, a prayer of confession, and a prayer of confidence unless you are also willing to pray a prayer of commitment. Prayer is no substitute for commitment. Prayer is not a smokescreen by which to hide a lack of commitment.

"You can do more than pray after you have prayed, but you cannot do more than pray until you have prayed" (S. D. Gordon, *Quiet Talks on Prayer*, Createspace Independent, 2013). Then you should take action. It will take all of us. It is not equal giving but equal sacrifice. Many in ministry do not want to get out of their warm nests. May our Lord help us to get out of warm nests and fly higher than ever before!

WE NEED TO ORGANIZE OUR COMMITMENT

Sooner or later, every leader will face overwhelming problems and daunting fears. When a person chooses to lead, they will have to learn to navigate in an uncharted land. As I have said before, "Old maps will not work in a new land." As we enter new lands, the Holy Spirit will also provide the insights necessary to be successful.

In addition to visualizing our circumstances and agonizing over our conditions, we need to organize our commitment as we continue to lay one brick upon another. People who do not have a plan will be subject to those who do have a plan. There are some people who get so spiritual they fail to do anything practical. Nehemiah was deeply spiritual yet intensely practical. When God began to move in his heart and he saw that the walls were in disarray, his mind began to work and he began to plan.

Just as Nehemiah made plans, we are also to make plans for our own lives and ministries. Our plans are to be soaked and saturated in prayer. As a result, we will know our plans are God's plans for we will have the mind of Christ and will be thinking His thoughts. Ultimately our paradigm or mindset will be formed and fashioned after the mindset of Christ.

There are some people who do not want to plan. They feel that if you organize, you are not spiritual. However, the opposite is true: You are unspiritual if you do not organize; you are unspiritual if you do not plan. God is a very practical God: *Let all things be done decently and in order* (1 Corinthians 14:40).

> *And it came to pass in the month of Nisan, in the twentieth year of King Artaxerxes, when wine was before him, that I took the wine and gave it to the king. Now I had never been sad in his presence before. Therefore the king said to me, "Why is your face sad, since you are not sick? This is nothing but sorrow of heart." So I became dreadfully afraid* (Nehemiah 2:1-2).

Why would he be so afraid to just look sad? Because no cupbearer — no servant at all — would dare to come into the presence of an oriental king with a sad face. It would be an unforgivable sin punishable by death. No wonder Nehemiah was afraid.

The king said, "You're not sick. Why are you looking so sad?" Nehemiah had a burden on his heart so big he could not hide it. What was on his heart came out on his face. Nehemiah had prayed and sought the face of God and said to the king, *"May the king live forever! Why should my face not be sad, when the city, the place of my fathers' tombs, lies waste, and its gates are burned with fire?" Then the king said to me, "What do you request?" So I prayed to the God of heaven* (Nehemiah 2:3-4).

The king said, "What is it you want, Nehemiah?"

Nehemiah was praying and talking at the same time. Have you ever done that? I do that when I preach. There are times when I am praying and preaching at the same time.

In essence, Nehemiah was saying, "Oh God, here's my chance. Lord, the king wants to know what it is I want."

Do you think he just suddenly blurted it out? For four months he had been planning it. He knew exactly what he wanted, and he asked three things of the king that every one of us need to ask.

We Need to Ask for God's Favor

The first thing he asked for was the king's favor or permission. *Then the king said to me, "What do you request?" So I prayed to the God of heaven. And I said to the king, "If it pleases the king, and if your servant has found favor in your sight, I ask that you send me to Judah, to the city of my fathers' tombs, that I may rebuild it"* (Nehemiah 2:4-5).

Before we do anything in the name of Jesus, we had better get His favor.

Before we do anything in the name of Jesus, we had better get His favor. It is as dangerous to run ahead of God as it is to run behind Him.

Someone might say that he did not need an earthly king's permission, yet it was not the earthly king who was giving him permission. We know that an earthly king is controlled by the heavenly King, the King of kings: *The king's heart is in the hand of the LORD, like the rivers of water; He turns it wherever He wishes* (Proverbs 21:1).

We Need to Ask for God's Fortitude

Furthermore I said to the king, "If it pleases the king, let letters be given to me for the governors of the region beyond the River, that they must permit me to pass through till I come to Judah (Nehemiah 2:7).

He was saying, "As I go, these people are going to say, 'Who are you?' and 'What is your authority? What right do you have to travel here?'" In addition, he requested "a letter that I can pull out. I want something that I can show to say that King Artaxerxes sent me. I want your protection."

As God's children, we have His divine fortitude. Aren't you glad He has given us His letter, God's Holy Word? Aren't you glad He has given us His authority? Jesus said, *Behold, I give you the authority to trample on serpents and scorpions, and over all the power of the enemy,* (Luke 10:19). *And lo, I am with you always,* even *to the end of the age* (Matthew 28:20).

We Need to Ask for God's Funding

He wanted the king's favor and the king's fortitude. He also wanted the king's funding. *And a letter to Asaph the keeper of the king's forest, that he must give me timber to make beams for the gates of the citadel which* pertains *to the temple, for the city wall, and for the house that I will occupy." And the king granted* them *to me according to the good hand of my God upon me* (Nehemiah 2:8). He was saying, "I need some building materials, king; and I want you to give them to me."

And the king granted them *to me according to the good hand of my God upon me* (Nehemiah 2:8). This earthly king was only a tool in the hand of the King of kings. *The king's heart* is *in the hand of the* LORD, *like the rivers of water; He turns it wherever He wishes* (Proverbs 21:1).

When we visualize until God gives us a burden and then if we will take that burden and agonize over it until we know that we have confessed our sins and made a commitment, then we have every right to come, organize, and go to work.

When we visualize until God gives us a burden and then if we will take that burden and agonize over it until we know that we have confessed our sins and made a commitment, then we have every right to come, organize, and go to work. We have every right to look into the face of our God and say, "God, I want your permission; I want your protection; and I want your provision because I am getting ready to rise up and build."

I am not just talking about building a building; I am talking about building a life, a family, relationships. It is time for God's people to begin to act like it: *The people who know their God shall be strong, and carry out great exploits* (Daniel 11:32). Let's go out and do great and amazing exploits in the name of Lord!

2

THE WINNING SIXFOLD STRATEGY FOR SUCCESS

So I came to Jerusalem and was there three days. Then I arose in the night, I and a few men with me; I told no one what my God had put in my heart to do at Jerusalem; nor was there any animal with me, except the one on which I rode. And I went out by night through the Valley Gate to the Serpent Well and the Refuse Gate, and viewed the walls of Jerusalem which were broken down and its gates which were burned with fire. Then I went on to the Fountain Gate and to the King's Pool, but there was no room for the animal under me to pass (Nehemiah 2:11-14).

These principles in Nehemiah will be true in the building of our lives. We have a family to build, and these principles will be true in the building of our family. We have a business to build, and these principles will be true in the building of our business. We have a Global Church Network to build, and these principles will be true here as well.

Nehemiah had received a commission from the Lord to rebuild the walls of Jerusalem that were in decay and broken down and fallen, leaving the people of God without defense and in despair.

As we continue in *The Winning Qualities of High Impact Leaders*, we want to explore six principles that Nehemiah practiced in building the walls. We just discussed three steps to developing a winning mindset over the problems in life. Now we want to discuss and learn to apply six powerful principles of building great success in our lives. Nehemiah was one of the greatest leaders who ever lived. Both his words and his works will teach us how to know the Lord's will for our life and how to lead others into His will and on to victory.

PRINCIPLE ONE:
PRACTICE OUR REFOCUS

The very first thing Nehemiah did was to practice his refocus: *Then I arose in the night, I and a few men with me; I told no one what my God had put in my heart to do at Jerusalem; nor was there any animal with me, except the one on which I rode* (Nehemiah 2:12).

We have a business to build, and these principles will be true in the building of our business.

Nehemiah had a mandate from God. Nehemiah was a man who knew how to get alone with God. We must remember that he fasted, he prayed, and he wept; and God had told him what to do.

Have you done that? Have you gotten a leadership vision from the Lord, or are you just wandering aimlessly like a ship without a rudder, like a ship without a compass, like a ship without a sail? Are you just putting yourself in neutral and letting life push you around, or do you have a focus, a goal, an aim?

God has a plan for your life; He has something He wants you to do. You are special to God; He made you just like He wants you. God has a specific job for you to do, and the same God who has called you is the same God who has equipped you with the talents to get it done. You cannot do what I do; I cannot do what you do; you cannot do what they do; and they cannot do what you do. However, God has a job for everyone; He has a plan for every life. I challenge you to get alone and fix your focus on that plan to find the will of God for your life!

One of the most strategic things we can ever do to help garner our success is to do thorough research.

Too many people are simply drawing their breath and drawing their salary without a plan or a goal. They get up in the morning, gulp down a cup of coffee, check their email, fight the traffic to work, work all day, come home, take an aspirin, watch the news, eat their dinner, watch a little television, and go to bed. The next day, it starts all over again. That is their life. However, God has something greater for you. Have you fixed your focus on the purpose of God?

Nehemiah said, "God had laid something on my heart." If you will listen, God will lay something on your heart, and He wants you to focus on it. We need to be like the Apostle Paul: *This one thing I do* (Philippians 3:13). Do you really have a goal in life? If not, why not? God has a purpose for your life, and your goal ought to be that purpose.

A person with a clear goal will have far more success than the person who does not have a goal who will always be subject to someone who has a goal for their life. Think about it.

PRINCIPLE TWO:
PURSUE OUR RESEARCH

One of the most strategic things we can ever do to help garner our success is to do thorough research. Over the years, I have watched fellow leaders try to duplicate what someone else has already done. I watch as they take another leader's ideas and try to bring them into a completely different culture. Most of time, these leaders fail because they are not willing to do the necessary research to figure out why and how the leader they are copying decided to do what they did to accomplish their success. Additionally, they do not know how many times the other leader failed before discovering the missing ingredient for success in their lives. The greater the research, the greater the rewards!

> *And I went out by night through the Valley Gate to the Serpent Well and the Refuse Gate, and viewed the walls of Jerusalem which were broken down and its gates which were burned with fire. ¹Then I went on to the Fountain Gate and to the King's Pool, but* there was *no room for the animal under me to pass. So I went up in the night by the valley, and viewed the wall; then I turned back and entered by the Valley Gate, and so returned* (Nehemiah 2:13-15).

What is Nehemiah doing? He is riding on a horse in the middle of the night gathering all the facts. He wants to see what the condition really is for the people of God. He is not like an ostrich that sticks its head in the sand. He is saying, "Really, what are the facts?" and once he sees these facts, he is then ready to go and do God's work.

What were the facts that he saw? He saw that God's work was in ruins and in shambles. He saw that the walls around the city of Jerusalem that had been a thing of strength and beauty and a thing that brought glory to God were torn down and destroyed.

What does that mean to us today? The walls of orthodoxy have crumbled, and Satan has developed a juiceless, polished type of preacher who has substituted culture for Calvary and reformation for regeneration.

We have satanic cults that have been vomited up out of the pit of hell. These people are going from house to house and door to door using the Master's method and the devil's message. They are set on fire from hell and filled with deadly poison.

We are living in a money-motivated, sex-soaked, distorted age; and it no longer breaks our hearts.

Not only have the walls of orthodoxy crumbled, but the walls of decency have also crumbled. We are living in a money-motivated, sex-soaked, distorted age; and it no longer breaks our hearts. We simply overlook the sins that slink their way down the main streets of society.

In order for any leader to have maximum influence and impact in their culture, it is paramount that they determine the facts. We are not able to make correct decisions and measure our level of effectiveness until know we know the facts. We need to become a "spiritual" Nehemiah. I challenge you to go out and make a survey to find out for yourself what the situation is where you live and serve.

PRINCIPLE THREE:
PREPARE OUR RELATIONSHIPS

We must make the team work in order to make the dream work. The closest distance between two points is not a straight line but a close relationship. When we set out to accomplish significance with our lives, we will need a lot of key people around us. The people we choose to have around us will determine our level of success. If we have leaders who rank 7 on a scale of 10, we limit ourselves for the future. If we must fire someone, we need be sure to hire up the next time instead of hiring down.

These rock-solid principles will work in our family, our business, our ministry, or our organization.

Thus far, we have learned that we must refocus and do research. They both go hand in hand with effectiveness. The more we understand a "vision," the greater the focus will be in our hearts and minds.

Regardless as to whether you are just beginning a ministry or have to come to halftime in your life/ministry, these foundational principles are strategically important for future success.

> *Then I said to them, "You see the distress that we are in, how Jerusalem lies waste, and its gates are burned with fire. Come and let us build the wall of Jerusalem, that we may no longer be a reproach"* (Nehemiah 2:17).

Nehemiah did not believe in a one-man ministry. He knew there is strength in numbers and in unity. He knew he could not possibly do it by himself. Though God had called him to lead, he said, "Come, let us do it together." *For we are laborers together with God* (1 Corinthians 3:9 KJV). It is powerful when we work together in unity!

Canadian geese fly in a V-formation with the lead goose making it easier for all of the rest of them as it splits a way through the air, moving the wind resistance. While the lead goose is flapping its wings hard, the rest of the geese are "cruising." After a while, however, the lead goose gets tired and falls back to the end and the next goose moves up. The new lead goose then takes care of the resistance for a while.

Henry Ford, a mastermind of organization and cooperation, said, "Coming together is the beginning. Keeping together is progress. Working together is success.

Engineers who have studied wind tunnel experiments have found that geese, flying in a V-formation, can fly 72 percent farther than one goose can fly by itself.

What is God teaching us? The same thing that He has put into nature: We can do more together than any one of us can do by ourselves. How we need to work together!

While one shall chase a thousand, two shall chase ten thousand (Deuteronomy 32:30 KJV). It is time that we focus and say, "Together we build the kingdom of God!"

Henry Ford, a mastermind of organization and cooperation, said, "Coming together is the beginning. Keeping together is progress. Working together is success" (Goodreads.com/Henry Ford Quotes).

What great wisdom! I challenge you to write it down and pray over it for at least a month. There is something dynamic about forming a fellowship. No matter what you are doing, even if you are building your own personal life, you cannot do it by yourself. *For none of us lives to himself* (Romans 14:7). Your family—husband, wife, sons, daughters—has to do it together in order to build your family. If you have a business, you need to involve those people who are working for you—do it together, form a fellowship!

The first three principles can be summed up by refocus, research, and relationships!

PRINCIPLE FOUR:
PROVIDE OUR RENEWAL

What is renewal? What is faith? Is it hoping and waiting for something to happen? Is faith positive thinking? When does faith become faith? The Word of God says that *faith comes by hearing, and hearing by the word of God* (Romans 10:17). There are countless numbers of people who hear the Word of God, but do they have faith? Part of "having faith" is the hearing of the Word of God.

Faith is belief with legs on it. The Lord does not call us to sit, soak, and sour but stand in our faith. Faith becomes faith when we hear and then act on what the Lord has put in our heart.

On one occasion, Jesus said, *If you have faith as a mustard seed, you will say to this mountain, "Move from here to there," and it will move* (Matthew 17:20). How large is mustard seed faith? About the size of a fleck of pepper. What is Jesus teaching? That it is not necessarily great faith in God but faith in a great God that makes the difference!

Notice what Nehemiah did. He fixed his focus; and after he fixed his focus, he found his facts. He went out and looked at the situation. After he examined it, he formed a fellowship. He gathered some people to him and said, "Folks, we're going to do it together, and it's going to be wonderful and it's going to be glorious!"

When it comes to rebuilding the walls of lives or ministry or building a Christ-centered or God-glorifying organization, sooner or later we will have to have our faith renewed in the Lord.

And I told them of the hand of my God which had been good upon me, and also of the king's words that he had spoken to me (Nehemiah 2:18). I love this verse. I want God's hand to be good upon me, don't you? *And I told them of the hand of my God which had been good upon me, and also of the king's words that he had spoken to me.*

What had the king spoken unto him? First, he had the king's favor. Second, he had the king's fortitude. Third, he had the king's funding. From the King of kings, we have His favor, His fortitude, and His funding. Nehemiah simply rehearsed what the king had said to him and how the hand of God was good upon him!

What was he to do next? He knew they needed to be fortified in their faith. He knew human nature fears the new. Whenever anybody says, "Let us rise and do something great and noble," there's always a sick feeling in the pit of our stomach that maybe it cannot be done.

If God is leading, if God's good hand is upon us, then it can be done.

If God is leading, if God's good hand is upon us, then it can be done. Nehemiah turned around for a little bit and reviewed the past so that he could face the future. He was saying that the God of yesterday is the God of tomorrow.

The LORD has done great things for us, and we are glad (Psalm 126:3). God has done great things! He is the God of yesterday, today, and tomorrow. He is the same great God. Nehemiah just reviewed the hand of God that had been upon them. I think of the hand of God upon us together around the world.

Why is God blessing? Does God just bless arbitrarily? Does God just bless sometimes because it is a whim or a fancy? No, the God who formed this universe works according to principles; and if you want to know why the hand of God was upon Nehemiah or why the hand of God is upon any church or ministry, you can find it in the Bible.

Revelation 3:7-8 tells the story of the church at Philadelphia. Sometimes I wonder why some churches grow and are blessed and why God sets before them an open door while others seem to have a closed door. Is it because God has favorites? I think not; however, I do believe He has intimates.

When the Lord places a vision in your heart
to move the Church forward toward
the fulfillment of the Great Commission,
the enemy will do all he can stop you.

To the angel of the church in Philadelphia write, 'These things says He who is holy, He who is true, "He who has the key of David, He who opens and no one shuts, and shuts and no one opens" (Revelation 3:7). Our God is the keeper of the keys; and when He opens a door, there are not enough demons in hell to shut it. Conversely, when He shuts a door, there are not enough angels in heaven to kick it open.

Our Lord is the one who opens and closes doors in our personal lives, in our businesses, in our families, and in our churches. He is the one who opens what no one can shut and shuts what no one can open.

Does God do this on a whim? Absolutely not. God set before that church an open door when He told them, *I know your works* (Revelation 3:8). Here was a church that was activated by the Spirit of God. "I know your works."

It was a working church. God is not going to bless indolence/laziness. God only opens doors for people who want to go through them. Philadelphia was a church that was activated by the Spirit of God.

You…have kept my word (Revelation 3:8). Not only were they activated by the Spirit of God, but they were also saturated with the Word of God. It was a church that loved God's Word. It was a Word-believing, Word-preaching church.

However, there is one more thing: *You…have not denied my name* (Revelation 3:8). They were dedicated to the Son of God.

To a church that is activated by the Spirit of God, saturated by the Word of God, and dedicated to the Son of God, He says, "I will give to that church, that person, that family, that business an open door! And when I open that door, no one can shut it; and when I shut it, no one can open it."

I believe that is the reason that Nehemiah, even in the Old Testament, had the good hand of God upon him. God does not act capriciously. God acts according to certain principles. Do you want God to open a door in your personal life, in your business, in your home, in your soul winning? God works and God acts according to powerful, proven principles.

PRINCIPLE FIVE:
PLAN OUR RESISTANCE

In a letter to Jerome Weller in July 1530, Martin Luther, the founder of the Protestant Reformation, said, "For where God built a church, there the Devil would also build a chapel." When the Lord places a vision in your heart to move the Church forward toward the fulfillment of the Great Commission, the enemy will do all he can stop you;

but our Lord specializes in turning dead ends into four-lane highways for our good and for His glory.

We have witnessed Nehemiah's "getting a word from God" and then going out to accomplish what he has been told to do. We have learned how to turn problems into possibilities. Once we get into a position of possibilities, then these possibilities can become certainties in the hands of God.

Once we have learned how to develop a winning mindset to overcome, we need to learn and be able to apply the leadership principles of building godly significance in our lives and ministries. We have learned thus far to refocus, research, relationships, and renewal. At this point, we must get prepared to Plan Our Resistance.

> *But when Sanballat the Horonite, Tobiah the Ammonite official, and Geshem the Arab heard of it, they laughed at us and despised us, and said, "What is this thing that you are doing? Will you rebel against the king?" So I answered them, and said to them, "The God of heaven Himself will prosper us; therefore we His servants will arise and build, but you have no heritage or right or memorial in Jerusalem"* (Nehemiah 2:19-20).

Whether in personal life or corporate life, anytime God's people say, "Let us rise up and build," all the hosts of hell will say, "Let us rise up and stop them." The door to the room of opportunity swings on the hinges of opposition. If you think there is an easy way, a cheap way, a lazy way to do the work of God, forget it. The Apostle Paul said, *For a great and effective door has opened to me, and* there are *many adversaries* — many adversaries (1 Corinthians 16:9 Emphasis added).

An open door does not mean there are no adversaries. When God calls us to do this something great with Him, do you think it is going to be easy? It is not. Our Lord is not calling us to a Sunday school picnic but to a grim conflict.

Nehemiah was confronted by three wicked, demon-inspired men who represented the devil himself. We are coming against the demonized, mobilized forces of hell in this world. Whenever we decide to do anything great and noble and good, there will be plenty of people who will say, "Let's stop them! Let's stop them!" They do not like anything that is built for the name of Jesus and the cause of Christ.

When God calls us to do this something great with Him, do you think it is going to be easy?

Think of the names the Bible gives to the devil: deceiver, liar, murderer, accuser, tempter, destroyer, the evil one. These things are enough to tell us something about the character of the one who opposes us. However, opposition ought not to discourage us; it ought to encourage us.

I have learned a little secret. Whenever I go to minister or travel a long distance to serve in the work of the Lord, "things happen"—things for which you cannot plan. People will say terrible, negative things; or a lot of problems will come my way. If we are not careful, these "things" can bother us. However, we need to realize that the devil is upset. Think about this: Would you rather be a person who is living the kind of life that makes the devil mad or the kind of life that makes the devil think you are no threat to him or his dark kingdom?

If God is for us, who can be against us? (Romans 8:31). *He who is in you is greater than he who is in the world* (1 John 4:4). Have you fixed your focus on that thing which God has called you to do? Have you found the facts? Have you formed a fellowship? Have you fortified your faith? Have you faced your foe? Do not worry about your foe; let him be an encouragement to you. If there are people who say something bad about you, do not worry about it. Learn to move past it.

---

*Each of us are called by our Lord
to fulfill our divine destiny during the time
we have upon the earth.*

How can you escape criticism? They will criticize you for saying nothing, doing nothing, and being nothing. They will criticize you if say something, do something, or become something. There is no way you are going to escape criticism; forget that notion. There will always be a Sanballat, a Geshem, or an Arabian to say, "What do you think you're up to? What do you think you're doing?" Face your foe with faith and move forward with the Lord!

PRINCIPLE SIX:
PERCEIVE OUR REWARD

In 1915, Leon Trotsky, one of the leaders of the Bolshevik Revolution and the spread of communism, was invited to a Sunday School class in Chicago. He went to the class because he was searching, looking for ideas. When Trotsky came to that class, the Sunday school teacher was not even there; he never showed up. Furthermore, he had not appointed anyone to take his place. As far as history tells us, that was the last time Trotsky ever attended any kind of a Bible study or church.

In 1917, Trotsky was in the middle of the Bolshevik Revolution, leading what was changing the world and damning the souls of men. One cannot help but wonder what would have happened in 1915 if he had come into a Sunday School class where there had been a Spirit-filled, Bible-drilled, victory-thrilled man or woman of God teaching the class. What would have happened if there had been a person there with the anointing of God upon them? What may have happened on that day? God knows, but we will never know because there was a Sunday school teacher who had missed their place along the wall—and because of that, there was a gap.

Each of us are called by our Lord to fulfill our divine destiny during the time we have upon the earth. Thus far we have learned refocus, research, relationships, renewal, and resistance. We will now be challenged to perceive our reward!

Then Eliashib the high priest rose up with his brethren the priests and built the Sheep Gate; they consecrated it and hung its doors. They built as far as the Tower of the Hundred, and consecrated it, then as far as the Tower of Hananel. Next to Eliashib the men of Jericho built. And next to them Zaccur the son of Imri built. Also the sons of Hassenaah built the Fish Gate; they laid its beams and hung its doors with its bolts and bars (Nehemiah 3:1-3).

The rest of Chapter 3 shows us that everyone had a role in the goal; everyone had a part in the plan; every person fulfilled their function as each of them worked together to rebuild the wall. When all pertinent qualities come together, we will be able fulfill our function in our generation.

The Pattern to Practice

Notice the pattern to practice and how they did it. Each one of them found an organized spot—at least there was a leader. They did not just all go off and say, "Well, I'm going to do my thing." God had a plan and gave this plan through His spiritual leadership to the people. The people recognized God's chain of authority and were willing to follow God's man and do as he directed them.

Each person had a part in the work; each person had a job to do. No one person can do everything, but everyone can do something. I cannot do everything, but I can do something. What I can do, I ought to do; and what I can do and ought to do, that, by the grace of God, I will do. There was a principle: not equal gifts but equal sacrifice.

The People of Purpose

There was a job for everyone: apothecaries, goldsmiths, and priests were working. Some of them were young; some were old. Some of them were rulers; some were laborers; some were craftsmen. The rich were there; the poor were there. Women and men were all doing their part.

Each person had a part in the work; each person had a job to do. No one person can do everything, but everyone can do something.

We will never get 100 percent to work: *Next to them the Tekoites made repairs; but their nobles did not put their shoulders to the work of their Lord* (Nehemiah 3:5). Notice again: *Their nobles did not put their shoulders to the work of their Lord.* There are always some people like that—always

34

some who sit back and say, "Well, if they want to do it, just let them do it."

These are days of opportunity — golden days, glorious days. Do not miss them! Do not let the final record be written of you that when these great days — so rich with opportunity — were upon us, you did not have a part in them! God forbid that should be forever written about you!

The Places to Perform

Everyone started building right near their own house. We must start with our family first. We must pray together and discover what each family member will do in the kingdom of God.

Each of us can work together to build something of significance with our Lord. We can either be part of it or watch others build it without us.

We must start with our own house, in our own heart, in our own life. Each of us must live our lives in step with God. We must get alone with God and get on our knees and say, "Oh God, make my heart right! And if nobody else does anything, Lord, I want to be your person. I want to be found faithful."

Each of us must find our place along the wall. What is your place? What has God called you to be and do in this generation?

We are either a stumbling block or a stepping-stone. *The God of heaven Himself will prosper us; therefore we His servants will arise and build, but you have no heritage or right or memorial in Jerusalem* (Nehemiah 2:20).

Each of us can work together to build something of significance with our Lord. We can either be part of it or watch others build it without us. We can either step through the door of opportunity into a victorious room or watch the door close in front of us.

We have learned to practice our refocus, pursue our research, prepare our relationships, provide our renewal, plan our resistance, and perceive our reward.

3

THE WINNING RULES
AGAINST RIDICULE

We need to remember that Nehemiah was God's man. He was commissioned by the Lord to go back to Jerusalem to help the Jews rebuild their torn down walls that were in disgrace and disrepair.

> *But it so happened, when Sanballat heard that we were rebuilding the wall, that he was furious and very indignant, and mocked the Jews. And he spoke before his brethren and the army of Samaria, and said, "What are these feeble Jews doing? Will they fortify themselves? Will they offer sacrifices? Will they complete it in a day? Will they revive the stones from the heaps of rubbish — stones that are burned?" Now Tobiah the Ammonite was beside him, and he said, "Whatever they build, if even a fox goes up on it, he will break down their stone wall." Hear, O our God, for we are despised; turn their reproach on their own heads, and give them as plunder to a land of captivity! Do not cover their iniquity, and do not let their sin be blotted out from before You; for they have provoked You to anger before the builders. So we built the wall, and the entire wall was joined together up to half its height, for the people had a mind to work* (Nehemiah 4:1-6).

The devil wants to stop any work for God; and when God's people say, "Let us arise and build," all the host of hell says, "Let us arise and stop them." We would perhaps be amazed to know that one of Satan's chief tools is ridicule. We may think that ridicule is something we can just toss off; however, ridicule is one of the hardest things we will ever face as a Christian. The servant is not better than his master. If they ridiculed the Lord Jesus Christ, they are going to ridicule us. When we make up our minds to build an extraordinary ministry or business to the glory of the Lord, sooner or later, ridicule will come our way.

WE MUST LEARN THE RESPONSE
TO RIDICULE

When we commit our time and resources to building something great for our Lord, people (both Christians and non-Christians) will find ways to try to tear down with words what we are building with work and worship. Sooner or later, criticism and ridicule will find us!

The Feebleness of Our People

The first thing they ridiculed was the feebleness of God's people: *And he spoke before his brethren and the army of Samaria, and said, "What are these feeble Jews doing?* (Nehemiah 4:2).

We would perhaps be amazed to know that one of Satan's chief tools is ridicule.

We are a feeble people if we look at it according to the world's standards. The world measures things by numbers, size, prestige, and finances. They look at us and think of the church and the Church worldwide as just a feeble little group. They are not very impressed with us because the world is impressed by size and prestige.

Sanballat was saying, "Ha, ha! Look at them—feeble people!" The world makes the mistake of measuring Christianity by the size of the people. We may not look like much, but the Bible says God has chosen the weak things of this world to confound the wise and the mighty. We are laughed at sometimes because of our feebleness.

The Futility of Our Project

Nehemiah and his team were laughed at because of the futility of the task: *Will they complete it in a day? Will they revive the stones from the heaps of rubbish — stones that are burned?* (Nehemiah 4:2). In other words, they will never do what they say they are going to do; it just cannot be done. It may look like we have a futile task; however, we are going to win. We cannot lose; we will prevail.

"I had rather temporarily lose with a cause that must ultimately succeed, than temporarily succeed with a cause that must ultimately fail."

Woodrow Wilson said, "I had rather temporarily lose with a cause that must ultimately succeed, than temporarily succeed with a cause that must ultimately fail" (Goodreads.com/Woodrow Wilson Quotes). The Church will win!

The Foolishness of Our Praise

They also mocked the foolishness of their faith and praise: *Will they offer sacrifices?* (Nehemiah 4:2). Now he is mocking their religion—their very faith. *For the message of the cross is foolishness to those who are perishing* (1 Corinthians 1:18).

People laugh at the things we preach. They hear us preaching about a crucified Christ and our magnificent Savior, and they laugh.

The Frailty of Our Progress

They laughed at the frailty of their progress: *Whatever they build, if even a fox goes up on it, he will break down their stone wall* (Nehemiah 4:3). That is, a little ole fox crawling over their stone wall is going to break it down. That is, it is not going to last. And again, the world mocks and laughs. That is what the world says—it will not last. People will laugh at your early beginnings. Let them laugh! Keep on building!

The devil has not changed his tactics. He is still mocking, still laughing. If you are doing a work for God, you might as well get ready: You are going to face some ridicule.

WE MUST LEARN THE REFLECTIONS OF REDICULE

We are learning how to rebuild the walls in our generation. Over the years, much has been written about Nehemiah and his leadership approaches to great success. We learned that our enemy's approaches over the centuries have remained the same. We must be able to move past the rottenness of ridicule to our reflections of ridicule. *Hear, O our God; for we are despised* (Nehemiah 4:4).

Christians are despised today. When you are despised and mocked, consider several reflections to your ridicule.

The Cause for Our Ridicule

Do you know why the world laughs at Christians? Because ridicule is a substitute for reason and laughing is a substitute for logic. If they cannot reason us out of a work for God, they will try to ridicule us out of a work for God. If they cannot logic us out of a work for God, they will try to laugh us out of a work for God.

Do you know why the world laughs at Christians? Because ridicule is a substitute for reason and laughing is a substitute for logic.

If I had a dollar for every time I have heard someone laugh about the work we are doing, I would be a very wealthy person. Sooner or later, you must become deaf to the doubts of others and become determined to show them how great and glorious our God is. The fastest way to overcome ridicule is to go out and be successful!

The Character of Ridicule

We need to consider the character of those doing the ridiculing. We are known not only by the friends that we make but also by the enemies that we make. There would be something wrong with us if some people were not laughing at us.

In Acts 5:41, the disciples had been persecuted and departed from the presence of the council and rejoiced that they were counted worthy to suffer shame for His name.

You may say, "Nobody ever laughs at me." Keep it a secret! You have not yet been counted worthy. There is not enough in your life to make a difference.

When I think of business professionals, I want to tell them there is no way they can live for Jesus Christ in their profession without some of their compatriots and peers looking down on them and laughing at them.

When I think of college students, I want to tell them there is no way they can live a separated, godly, righteous life, carrying their Bible to class, bowing their head in the cafeteria, and praying without somebody pointing a finger of scorn at them.

There is no way we can share a testimony for the Lord Jesus Christ without somebody laughing at us. If they do not laugh at us, it is simply because we have not yet been counted worthy. Remember that when you go all out for God, you are going to face the godless gang and the Christless clique.

The Company of Ridicule

Consider the company you are in. Jesus was also scorned, and the servant is not better than his master. The following verses should not only break your heart but also encourage you at the same time.

Mark 5:40 (KJV). Jesus Christ is getting ready to perform one of his most notable miracles. Every time I read this, I can hardly believe it literally happened, but I know it did because the Bible says so: *And they laughed him to scorn*. Laughed whom to scorn? Jesus. They laughed him to scorn. They laughed in the face of the Son of God.

Luke 22:63. Our Lord Jesus Christ is in the hands of the soldiers: *Now the men who held Jesus mocked Him and beat Him.* I believe it was easier for Jesus to take the fisticuffs and the clubs that beat upon his head than to take the laughter and ridicule to his face. They mocked him, and they beat him.

Luke 23:35. *And the people stood looking on. But even the rulers with them sneered, saying, "He saved others; let Him save Himself if He is the Christ, the chosen of God."* Sneered...they ridiculed him; they laughed at him; they scorned him.

Luke 23:36. *The soldiers also mocked Him, coming and offering Him sour wine.* We must not allow the devil to laugh us out of a work for God.

The Compensation of Ridicule

We need to consider the compensation we are going to get for being laughed at. The Lord is going to pay us; do not worry about it. Jesus said: *Blessed are you when they revile and persecute you, and say all kinds of evil against you falsely for My sake. Rejoice and be exceedingly glad, for great is your reward in heaven, for so they persecuted the prophets who were before you* (Matthew 5:11-12). If people laugh at you all day, you just go home and laugh all night. We need to rejoice and be exceedingly glad for "great is our reward in heaven."

The Conclusion of Ridicule

Consider the conclusion of the whole matter of ridicule. You know what is said about he who laughs last: He who laughs last lasts best. So who going to have the last laugh? You say the Church. No. God himself. You can laugh your way right into hell, but you cannot laugh your way out. It is God, not man, who will have the last laugh.

Thomas Paine, the skeptic and infidel, asked Benjamin Franklin, "Ben, what do you think of my book, *The Age of Reason*" which was a book that ridiculed the Christian faith. Ben Franklin said, "Tom, when a man spits against the wind, he spits in his own face" (Goodreads.com/ Benjamin Franklin Quotes).

Consider the conclusion of the whole matter of ridicule. You know what is said about he who laughs last: He who laughs last lasts best.

Agathon was a young Roman who had a boyhood friend name Julian. Agathon and Julian grew up together and played together. Julian grew up to become the emperor of Rome and was known as an apostate emperor. He was cruel and hated Christ and Christians and did all he could to put down Christianity.

One day after both men were grown, Julian met Agathon. Trying to taunt Agathon for his faith, Julian asked him, "How is the carpenter of Nazareth doing these days? Is he getting plenty of work? Is there enough work to keep your carpenter busy?" Agathon said, "Yes, Julian, the carpenter is getting plenty of work. Today he is nailing together a coffin to put your empire in." Agathon served to be a prophet because within two years, Julian was slain by the Persians and his empire was crumbling.

It is God who will get the last laugh. We need to consider why we are being ridiculed, who is doing the ridiculing, who along with us is being ridiculed, what is God going to pay us for being ridiculed, and what is the conclusion of the whole matter. We must not let anyone laugh us out of a work for God.

We have been learning about the rottenness of ridicule and our reflections on it. Thus far, we have learned the enemy will ridicule the feebleness of our people, the futility of our project, the foolishness of our praise, and the frailty of our progress. When the rottenness of ridicule sets in, we must know how to reflect and not react to it. To combat this ridicule, we should consider its cause, character, company, compensation, and conclusion.

WE MUST LEARN THE ROAD
THROUGH RIDICULE

Once we understand the rottenness of ridicule and undertake our reflection to ridicule, we are now on the road through ridicule.

Prayerful Intercession

There are two proactive steps forward to overcoming ridicule. We will desperately need prayerful intercession. Nehemiah's prayer: *Hear, O our God, for we are despised; turn their reproach on their own heads, and give them as plunder to a land of captivity! Do not cover their iniquity, and do not let their sin be blotted out from before You; for they have provoked You to anger before the builders* (4:4-5).

When the rottenness of ridicule sets in, we must know how to reflect and not react to it.

This is not a prayer for personal recrimination against them. Nehemiah is saying, "God, it is you they dishonor. You are the righteous judge. You get the glory to your name. Lord, they have provoked you to anger. When they are despising us, when they are laughing at us, Lord, they are laughing at you."

Notice what Nehemiah did. He did not get into a name-calling contest with them. We must stay above the name calling even if they call us names. A bulldog can whip a skunk, but it is not worth it. Nehemiah simply told God on them. Here they are laughing, mocking, scoffing, and ridiculing; and Nehemiah says, "Hear it, O God! Listen and take action!"

Surely He [God] *scorns the scornful, but gives grace to the humble* (Proverbs 3:34 Emphasis added. It is God who scoffs at the scoffers.

Who, when He was reviled, did not revile in return; when He suffered, He did not threaten, but committed Himself to Him who judges righteously (1 Peter 2:23). Peter was impressed by the way the Lord Jesus reacted to ridicule. When He was reviled, He reviled not again. He threatened not. He just told God on them. "Hear, O Lord!" We need to do that same thing today. We should carry the ridicule to God in prayer and tell the Lord about it.

Physical Involvement

We will also need physical involvement: *So we built the wall, and the entire wall was joined together up to half its height, for the people had a mind to work* (Nehemiah 4:6). They did not have a mind to cry or a mind to criticize or a mind to gossip, but they had a mind to work! Despite all the threats of the enemy and all the ridicule and scorn, they just started to do what God had called them to do.

Somebody said it could not be done; but with a chuckle, he replied that maybe it could not but he would not be one who would say so until he tried. So he buckled right in with the trace of a grin on his face; if he worried, he hid it.

He started to sing as he tackled the thing that could not be done.

We are not saved by works; we are saved by the grace of God: *For by grace you have been saved through faith, and that not of yourselves; it is the gift of God, not of works, lest anyone should boast* (Ephesians 2:8-9).

Good works cannot save us. Salvation is in the mercy of God, not in the merit of man.

Good works cannot save us. Salvation is in the mercy of God, not in the merit of man. It is in the grace of God, not in the goodness of man. Salvation is not a prize we receive at the end of the race; it is a gift that enables us to run the race. The moment I trusted the Lord Jesus Christ, God saved me. It is not of works; I cannot work my soul to be saved. This work was done by my Lord. I will work like any slave for the love of God's Son.

The people had a mind to work. Do you have a mind to do God's work? If so, let's get started building the walls of grace throughout every nation on earth!

4

THE WINNING ANTIDOTES FOR DISCOURAGEMENT

All of us are wall builders. The walls in our lives represent protection, separation, and identification. We need walls. We need walls to protect our families and to protect our faith. We need walls to protect our future. We need walls of defense, walls of doctrine, walls of decency, and walls of duty. However, as we rise up to build, the devil will try to stop us; and one of our enemy's greatest tools is discouragement.

> *So we built the wall, and the entire wall was joined together up to half its height, for the people had a mind to work. Now it happened, when Sanballat, Tobiah, the Arabs, the Ammonites, and the Ashdodites heard that the walls of Jerusalem were being restored and the gaps were beginning to be closed* [that is, the open places began to be filled in] *that they became very angry and all of them conspired together to come and attack Jerusalem and create confusion. Nevertheless we made our prayer to our God, and because of them we set a watch against them day and night. Then Judah said, "The strength of the laborers is failing, and there is so much rubbish that we are not able to build the wall"* (Nehemiah 4:6-10 Emphasis added).

As the people were at the halfway point of rebuilding the walls, somebody came with a report saying, "We can't do it. We're tired. We're worn out. The job is too big." As a result, they got discouraged.

When God's people have a mind to work,
the devil has a mind to wreck.

Do you ever get discouraged? Of course, you do. All of us from time to time get discouraged. I am so grateful for the Book of Nehemiah which has been a constant encouragement to me as a fellow-leader through the years. If you feel so low that you could just sit on the curb and dangle your feet, pay attention because there is a way up. There are some powerful ways to get back up when you are down.

When God's people have a mind to work, the devil has a mind to wreck. One of the ways Satan will keep you from being what you ought to be in your family, your business, your physical health, your Bible study, your soul-winning, or whatever is to come against you with discouragement.

All discouragement is of Satan or self; it is never of God. God is called the *God of all comfort* (2 Corinthians 1:3). That word comfort means "cancellation" or "encouragement." God has cornered the market on encouragement; and the devil who works against God works with discouragement.

If you are discouraged with your child, your marriage, your job, your service, or your health, the cause and the cure for that discouragement is in Nehemiah Chapter 4.

THERE ARE FOUR DISTINCT CAUSES FOR DISCOURAGMENT

The first reason the people who were rebuilding the walls got discouraged was simply because they were worn out. It was a problem of fatigue.

Then Judah said, "The strength of the laborers is failing" (Nehemiah 4:10). They were tired of carrying the load.

Fatigue: We Can Become Tired (Nehemiah 4:10)

We must admit it. As human beings, we are going to get tired. Jesus Christ himself got so tired that He sat on the curbing of a well when his disciples went to get food. Another time, Jesus Christ, the Lord of Glory, got so tired that He went to sleep in the back of a ship during a storm. No matter who we are, we can get physically tired. *Even the youths shall faint and be weary, and the young men shall utterly fall* (Isaiah 40:30).

If we get physically tired, we are set up to be discouraged. Sometimes the most spiritual thing we can do is to go to bed and sleep! If we burn the candle at both ends, we are not as bright as we think we are.

If we get physically tired, we are set up to be discouraged. Sometimes the most spiritual thing we can do is to go to bed and sleep!

When does discouragement come? *So we built the wall, and the entire wall was joined together up to half its height* (Nehemiah 4:6). When the job is half done is when we tend to get discouraged and when our strength seems to wear out. If you ever decide to climb a mountain, you will feel led to go back when you are halfway up! At that point, the newness of the adventure has worn off; and the second half of the journey seems so long. When you buy a new car, that new car smell is wonderful; but when you get it half paid for, you wonder if you ever should have bought it in the first place.

The people in Nehemiah Chapter 4 were worn out. It was a problem of fatigue. One of the great football coaches of all time, Vince Lombardi, said, "Fatigue makes cowards of us all" (https://www.48days.com/fatigue-makes-cow-ards-of-us-all). The number one reason you might get discouraged: You just may be tired.

Frustration: We Can Become Troubled (Nehemiah 4:10)

Not only were the rebuilders of the walls tired, but they were also troubled. *The strength of the laborers is failing, and there is so much rubbish* (Nehemiah 4:10). In order to rebuild the walls, the people had to use the old stones that had made up the original walls. They had to dig through the rubbish to find the stones, and they had to remove the rubbish to rebuild.

They were not just tired; they were also troubled. The task was not glamorous. It is not glamorous to dig through rubbish looking for stones. All of us have lives that collect rubbish! There is organizational rubbish, moral rubbish, theological rubbish, traditional rubbish, emotional rubbish, financial rubbish, and ministry rubbish! In order to rebuild, we must sort through all these kinds of rubbish; and the process can weigh us down!

You may be facing a situation or a task that seems too big for you. Your problem is not only fatigue but also frustration. You are not only worn out but also weighed down. It just seems like you will never get it finished. "The job is too big; it cannot be done." If you are discouraged, get alone with the Lord, spend some time with the greatest encouragers you know, and get some emotional and physical rest!

It is when we are halfway up a mountain or halfway through accomplishing a huge project that we are the most vulnerable to being attacked with the arrows of discouragement. Sooner or later when we are scaling our personal Everest or our ministry Everest, fatigue and frustration begin to tell us that we will not succeed — that we cannot fulfill the dream the Lord has placed in our hearts.

Long-distance runners know that when fatigue sets in, if they can just push through it, the power of the "second wind" will take them to the finish line.

What we need is a second wind. Long-distance runners know that when fatigue sets in, if they can just push through it, the power of the "second wind" will take them to the finish line.

Halftime in life is an important time; it is the time when we realize that we have lived at least half of our life on earth. During the halftime season, in order to avoid discouragement, we must make the right long-term decisions, take extra care of ourselves, and pray for the second wind to take us to the finish line.

We have come to a very important leadership intersection in life. There have been times when I have personally experienced all the lessons I am sharing with you. I am teaching out of the empathic overflow of my own life.

Fear: We Can Be Terrified (Nehemiah 4:11)

We can be tired — that is fatigue; we can be troubled — that is frustration. Then on the heels of these two, we can become fearful. *And our adversaries said, "They will neither know nor see anything, till we come into their midst and kill them and cause the work to cease"* (Nehemiah 4:11).

Nehemiah and his team were in actual physical danger. As a result of this, they were emotionally worked up and fearful.

If you feel as though there is a lot of negative stuff coming at you, it just may be that you are over the target. Satan will come against you. Jesus said, *Remember the word that I said to you, "A servant is not greater than his master." If they persecuted Me, they will also persecute you* (John 15:20). If you are not being persecuted, I wonder why not.

Satan is a clever, masterful deceiver. He knows when you are worn out and when you are weighed down. It is at that time that he comes to get you wrought up as well. It is at that time that he makes all kinds of threats against you. When the problems of fatigue, frustration, and fear begin to come together, you can become discouraged.

Failure: We Can Be Terminated (Nehemiah 4:11-12)

There is one other cause of discouragement that we see in Nehemiah's story. Not only were the people tired — that is fatigue, not only were they troubled — that is frustration, and not only were they terrified — that is fear; but they were also feeling a sense of termination — that is failure.

And our adversaries said, "They will neither know nor see anything . . . So it was, when the Jews who dwelt near them came, that they told us ten times, "From whatever place you turn, they will be upon us." (Nehemiah 4:11-12).

It is terrible enough when our enemies say it cannot be done; but when our friends say it cannot be done, that is ten times worse! Ten times their teammates—those who were supposed to be on their side—said, "You can't do it." They said it over and over and over again: "You are a failure, Nehemiah. You will never get it done." If your closest friends are making you feel like a failure even though you know, without a doubt, that you have heard from God, then make the decision today to get some new faith-filled friends!

It is terrible enough when our enemies say it cannot be done; but when our friends say it cannot be done, that is ten times worse!

Over the years in ministry, there have been and still are naysayers on one side and many yeasayers on the other side. It has been a constant tug of war. I have watched people come with their own hidden agendas, disguised in different fashions. One by one they come, and one by one they leave. I remember as if it were yesterday a particular person applauding the effort in front of others in a meeting only to tell me privately by phone that he was against this global vision. He went as far as to threaten me and oppose me.

On another occasion, I witnessed a well-known person raising money for his organization in the Green Room at our Global Church Network event. I was so disappointed when I saw this person do this! I watched pastors and leaders make financial commitments in front of each other so as to not be outdone by someone else. Then when they left for home, they never did send one dollar of their commitment to us.

You may know exactly how long each of the steps may take; but at the end of the day, it is the compass that matters more than the clock!

I remember the night in December 2006, lying on the floor in an Orlando condominium we were leasing, my face in the carpet, broken, lonely, and fearful, asking the Lord what He wanted me to do with the vision He had placed in my mind and heart. It was in the middle of the darkness of that awful night that the Lord gave me a plan of execution. When I gained enough strength to rise to my feet, I decided to walk this vision out day by day by faith until it came to pass in my generation.

It is in moments like this that fatigue, frustration, fear, and failure will swirl around us, telling us to quit and go do something else. Sooner or later, every visionary leader will face this midnight hour of the soul. If no one has ever fought against you, then your vision is probably not worth fighting for!

In the time when the four horsemen of discouragement want to undermine your confidence in who you are and in whose you are, take a pen and a sheet of paper and become more focused than you have ever been in your life. In my dark hour, I "faith-tuned" a list of ten steps to global networking success. After I wrote them down, I continued to pray over them and rearranged several of them. Once

I knew exactly the sequence of the steps to take, I got up every day knowing exactly what to do. It did not matter what others did or did not do or what others said or did not say. I stayed on the steps before me.

You may know exactly how long each of the steps may take; but at the end of the day, it is the compass that matters more than the clock! I did not know exactly how long each step would take, but I knew that with the Lord's insight and the Holy Spirit's strength, each step would be accomplished, and network momentum would move us forward for years to come.

I am not implying that we no longer face challenges; rather, we continue to do so as we navigate our way through the diverse international landscape before us. I sense we have come to the halfway point in this network, and I am praying for a second wind to take us to the finish line. When we talk about the "finish line," we are believing for the Great Commission to be completed by 2030.

Are you at the halfway point in your life and ministry? Are the four horsemen of discouragement coming against you? If so, get alone with the Lord, ask Him to set your compass, pull faith-filled friends close to you, and trust the Holy Spirit for your second wind.

THERE ARE FOUR DIVINE CURES
FOR DISCOURAGEMENT

Robert Louis Stevenson told a story about some passengers who were on a ship during a tumultuous storm (*Treasure Island*, Cassell & Company, London, 1883). It seemed like the ship might be going down. The passengers, huddled below, whispered one to another, "Will we go down? Are we safe?"

One of the passengers said, "I've got to find out." He made his way across the heaving decks and up to the pilot house where the pilot of the ship stood with his hand on the wheel. The pilot, knowing the passenger was afraid, turned and smiled at him. The passenger made his way below and said, "We're going be all right. I've seen the face of the pilot, and he smiled at me."

What we need to do, especially in a storm, is to seek the face of God. We need to find the smile of God. Our Lord has sailed rougher seas than the ones we may be in today.

What is the cure for discouragement? If you are discouraged today by children, by your marriage, by your schedule, by your ministry, or by whatever, what is the cure?

Renew Our Strength (Nehemiah 4:21-22)

So we labored in the work, and half of the men held the spears from daybreak until the stars appeared. At the same time I also said to the people, "Let each man and his servant stay at night in Jerusalem, that they may be our guard by night and a working party by day." (Nehemiah 4:21-22). In other words: "Go lie down and get some rest!"

When you become worn out and the problem of fatigue sets in, you can become discouraged.

When you become worn out and the problem of fatigue sets in, you can become discouraged. In many cases, the cure may be as simple as this: You just need to rest. You may need to change your diet. You may need to get some exercise. You may need to go to the doctor and get a checkup. The issue may be physical or emotional. Maybe you need a checkup from the neck up!

There is an interesting story in the Old Testament about another man — a prophet named Elijah. Elijah was a man of God, yet one time he got so discouraged he wanted to die.

But he himself went a day's journey into the wilderness, and came and sat down under a broom tree. And he prayed that he might die, and said, "It is enough! Now, Lord, take my life, for I am no better than my fathers!" Then as he lay and slept under a broom tree, suddenly an angel touched him, and said to him, "Arise and eat." Then he looked, and there by his head was a cake baked on coals, and a jar of water. So he ate and drank, and lay down again. And the angel of the Lord came back the second time, and touched him, and said, "Arise and eat, because the journey is too great for you." So he arose, and ate and drank; and he went in the strength of that food forty days and forty nights as far as Horeb, the mountain of God (1 Kings 19:4-8).

Elijah had a pity party. He got so discouraged he said he wanted to die. Of course, he really did not mean that. He had just run cross-country to get away from Jezebel. If he had wanted to die, all he would have had to do was stand still, and Jezebel would have taken care of him. She would have already said, "I'm going to make you a foot shorter at the top. I'm going to take off your head."

But he was drinking from the intoxicating cup of self-pity. He was worn out. He had been without food; he had been without rest; he had been without sleep, so he got under a juniper tree and said, "Oh, I wish I could die." He even prayed to die.

We often thank God for answered prayer, but have you ever thanked God for unanswered prayer? Thank God, He does not always answer our prayers! Elijah said, "God, I want to die"; but God said, "You're not going to die; you're going to sleep. Lie down, son, and sleep." And then He said, "Wake up and eat." And then, "Lie down and sleep." And then once again, "Wake up and eat."

Perhaps you just need a vacation. You might need to take some time off and let some things go.

Elijah thought he was the only prophet of the Lord; but the Lord said, "You know, Elijah, I've got a lot of people around here besides you. I've got 450 people who haven't bowed their knee to Baal so go to sleep and get some rest."

It is vain for you to rise up early, to sit up late, to eat the bread of sorrows; for so He gives His beloved sleep (Psalm 127:2).

Let me share some advice: Never make a major decision when you are fatigued. Just do not do it. Never make a major decision when you are depressed. Just do not do it.

Let me share some advice: Never make a major decision when you are fatigued.

The reason some of us may get discouraged is simple: We have not been taking care of the temple God gave us. To the prophet who wanted to die, God said, "Just lie down and sleep." To the people who wailed, "We can't build the wall," Nehemiah said, "Work in the daytime; sleep in the nighttime. You may need some rest."

Rethink Our Strategy (Nehemiah 4:13-14)

In the late 19th century, there was an Italian economist named Pareto who became the namesake of the Pareto Principle which states that 20 percent of what you do produces 80 percent of the results.

Many times in our lives and ministries, we are dealing with things that really do not matter. We are dealing with the rubbish rather than the stones.

As a leader, there are important things that only we can do with the highest quality — things that will also bring the highest return on our time, talent, and treasure.

We limit ourselves if we believe we can do both: handle the rubbish and the stones. Every visionary leader, at some point or another, must learn to prioritize what they are best equipped to do and let others take care of the "rubbish." In the building or rebuilding of our walls, we must invest our time in those things that give us the biggest return.

As a leader, there are important things that only we can do with the highest quality — things that will also bring the highest return on our time, talent, and treasure. Make a list of these significant building stones and then arrange them in the order that will bring the greatest success.

After we have sequenced them for success, we must take the first step to lift the first stone to further build our wall of ministry. For some stones, we will need to make a short list of elements required to execute with excellence. As we go through this process, life will become simpler, time will be saved, and outcomes will multiply greatly in the days ahead.

In the Book of Nehemiah, everyone was saying, "It can't be done." The enemy was saying, "We're going to kill you." Even friends were saying, "You better stop, or you're going to get yourselves killed."

To these statements, Nehemiah responded, *Therefore I positioned men behind the lower parts of the wall, at the openings;*

and I set the people according to their families, with their swords, their spears, and their bows. And I looked, and arose and said to the nobles, to the leaders, and to the rest of the people, "Do not be afraid of them. Remember the LORD*, great and awesome, and fight for your brethren, your sons, your daughters, your wives, and your houses"* (4:13-14). And he then got the whole project reorganized. In essence, he said, "Evidently, we're doing this the wrong way. We need to make a change."

If you are discouraged in a task, it may not be that you are doing the wrong thing. It may be that you are doing the right thing in the wrong way and you simply need to rethink your strategy. Consider building "think-time" into your daily schedule. If you are discouraged, set aside an hour or two to think through the whole project. Determine what is the rubbish and figure out where the stones are that you need to build with going forward.

Nehemiah did not give up the goal; he just refocused. Do you have a God-given goal? Is it clear? When was the last time you stopped to sit down — not only to renew your strength but also to rethink your strategy?

I want to challenge you to spend some time alone. I personally find my solitude and think-time when I am walking along the beach at the ocean — praying, problem solving, and planning. I write down those items I think I ought to do, and I refocus. Make time to rethink your strategy. It is one of the great cures for discouragement.

Revive Our Spirit

When we consider the great inspirational leaders throughout the Old and New Testaments, Nehemiah definitely makes the list. He took on a most difficult task against high odds to accomplish a significant outcome in a short period of time. His leadership saved a lot of people and brought high regard back to Jerusalem.

In the 1940s, Corrie ten Boom and her family helped Jews escape the Nazi Holocaust and, by all accounts, saved nearly 800 lives. Cornelia "Corrie" ten Boom was born in 1892 near Amsterdam in Haarlem, The Netherlands, and grew up in a devoutly religious family. During World War II, she and her family harbored hundreds of Jews to protect them from arrest by Nazi authorities. Betrayed by a fellow Dutch citizen, the entire family was imprisoned. Corrie survived the concentration camp, started a worldwide ministry, and later told her story in a bestselling book, *The Hiding Place*.

Known as "Corrie" all her life, she was the youngest of four children having two sisters, Betsie and Nollie, and her brother, Willem. Their father, Casper, was a jeweler and watchmaker. Cornelia was named after her mother.

In May 1940, the German Blitzkrieg stormed though the Netherlands and the other Low Countries. Within months, the "Nazification" of the Dutch people began; and the quiet life of the ten Boom family was changed forever.

During the war, the ten Boom "Beje house" became a refuge for Jews, students, and intellectuals. The façade of the watch shop below made the apartment an ideal front for these activities. A secret room, no larger than a small wardrobe closet, was built into Corrie's bedroom behind a false wall. The space could hold up to six people, all of whom had to stand quiet and still. A crude ventilation system was installed to provide air for the occupants. When security sweeps came through the neighborhood, a buzzer in the house would signal danger, allowing the refugees a little over a minute to seek sanctuary in the hiding place.

Corrie ten Boom became a leader in the "Beje" resistance movement, overseeing a network of safe houses in the country. However, on February 28, 1944, a Dutch informant told the Nazis of the ten Booms' activities; and the Gestapo raided the home. The Nazis kept the house under surveillance; and by the end of the day, 35 people, including the entire ten Boom family, were arrested. Although German soldiers thoroughly searched the house, they did not find the half-dozen Jews safely concealed in the hiding place. The six stayed in the cramped space for nearly three days before being rescued by the Dutch underground.

All ten Boom family members were incarcerated, including Corrie's 84-year-old father, who soon died in the Scheveningen prison located near The Hague. Corrie was eventually released from the Ravensbrück concentration camp for reasons not completely known.

After the war, Corrie returned to the Netherlands; and in 1946, she began a worldwide ministry that took her to more than 60 countries. She received many tributes, including being knighted by the queen of the Netherlands. In 1971, she wrote *The Hiding Place*, telling the story of her experiences during World War II.

Just as Corrie ten Boom had to wrestle with fatigue, frustration, and fear, so did Nehemiah many centuries earlier. In *The Hiding Place*, it is clear that Corrie had to renew her strength, rethink her strategy, and revive her spirit along the way.

We have been learning about the cures for discouragement. Thus far, we have learned that for fatigue, we renew our strength; and for frustration, we rethink our strategy. However, in addition to a physical cure and an organizational cure, there is also a spiritual cure. We need to revive our spirit.

And I looked, and arose and said to the nobles, to the leaders, and to the rest of the people, "Do not be afraid of them—what is the cure for fear?—Remember the Lord, great and awesome [terrible…KJV]" (Nehemiah 4:14 Emphasis added).

That is one of the greatest verses in the Bible. I suggest you take out a pen and underline it: *Do not be afraid of them. Remember the Lord, great and [terrible].* The word terrible means "terrifying to your enemies." How do we revive our spirit? We need to remember the Lord.

If you are discouraged, just think of all that God has done for you. Count your many blessings and see how faithful God has been.

King David *strengthened himself in the LORD his God* (1 Samuel 30:6). You get discouraged; you encourage yourself in the Lord. The question is, how?

Think of God's Goodness Yesterday

Think of God's goodness in the past. If you are discouraged, just think of all that God has done for you. Count your many blessings and see how faithful God has been. Psychologists tell us that gratefulness is one of the healthiest emotions we can possibly have. It is almost impossible to be grateful and discouraged at the same time. Count your many blessings, remember God's goodness in the past, and think of God's closeness in the present.

Think of God's Closeness Today

After reflecting on God's goodness in the past, remember God's closeness in the present. If you are in the midst of a problem, remember the Lord. Is your problem greater than God? I encourage you to take some time to allow the Holy Spirit to renew your spirit. Invite Him to spark the flame of renewal in your spirit and to spread it to every area of your mind, body, and soul.

In Acts 4:23-31, we see that the early disciples were facing threats from the political powers of their day. I will not take the time to elaborate, but these disciples went back to *their own companions* (v. 23). They discussed what was taking place in their lives, pulled themselves together, and prayed to the Lord. After they prayed, they were refilled with the Holy Spirit; and when they were refilled, they had a "holy boldness" to go out and face their fears with great faith!

Think of God's Faithfulness for Tomorrow

As you revive your spirit, think not only of His goodness in the past and His closeness in the present but also think of His faithfulness in the future. He says, *Never will I leave you; never will I forsake you* (Hebrews 13:5 NIV). He also says, *I can do all things through Christ who strengthens me* (Philippians 4:13). Encourage yourself in the Lord!

Do you know what fear is? Fear is forgetting God. That is why Nehemiah told his people, *Don't be afraid of them. Remember the Lord* (Nehemiah 4:14 NIV).

For God has not given us a spirit of fear, but of power and of love and of a sound mind (2 Timothy 1:7). *The* LORD *is my light and my salvation; whom shall I fear? The* LORD *is the strength of my life; of whom shall I be afraid?* (Psalm 27:1).

For fatigue, renew your strength. For frustration, refocus your strategy. For fear, remember the Lord. If you are afraid, it is because you have taken your eyes off the Lord. Remember, as Nehemiah said, "We serve a great God."

Corrie ten Boom is known for this adage: "If you look at the world, you'll be distressed. If you look within, you'll be depressed. If you look at God, you'll be at rest" (*The Hiding Place*, Chosen Books, 1984). I encourage you to write down Corrie ten Boom's words and read them every day for the next month!

Resolve Our Success

We have been learning the causes and cures of discouragement. We have also been applying practical lessons to help us push forward and pull upward and out of the vortex of discouragement. If we are not careful, when the "four horsemen" of fatigue, frustration, fear, and failure march into our lives, we can become overwhelmed by the sounds of discouragement that fill our hearts and minds. Praise be to the Lord though for there are at least four cures to the four causes of discouragement.

If we are not careful, when the "four horsemen" of fatigue, frustration, fear, and failure march into our lives, we can become overwhelmed by the sounds of discouragement that fill our hearts and minds.

When you are fatigued, renew your strength. When you are frustrated, rethink your strategy. When you are fearful, renew your spirit. And in the midst of approaching failure, resolve your success.

When I use the term "approaching failure," it is not implied that we have failed or are about to fail. Rather, there are times when people bring "bad news" and try to make us feel that we will not succeed. The situation appears gloomy and doubtful. It is during this timeframe that we need a psychological cure to resolve our success.

You will never "feel" your way into a work,
but you can work your way into a feeling.

As we build or rebuild the walls of our organization or ministry, we will need strong spirits, straightforward strategies, and simple steps to move through the rubbish of our lives and truly build upon the stones of success. Once we have learned this cycle of personal success, we will be able to apply and reapply it throughout the rest of our lives and ministries.

> *And I looked, and arose and said to the nobles, to the leaders, and to the rest of the people, "Do not be afraid of them. Remember the Lord, great and awesome, and fight for your brethren, your sons, your daughters, your wives, and your houses." And it happened, when our enemies heard that it was known to us, and that God had brought their plot to nothing, that all of us returned to the wall, everyone to his work* (Nehemiah 4:14-15).

We need to say, "By the grace of God, I will succeed." That is not positive thinking; that is faith. First, we remember the Lord when we say this; and then we say, "I have victory in Jesus."

If you are discouraged today, hear me: It is always too soon to quit. Do not give in and do not give up. Why? Remember what is at stake. Nehemiah said, *Do not be afraid of them. Remember the Lord, great and awesome, and fight for your brethren, your sons, your daughters, your wives, and your houses* (4:14). In other words, "Yes, the situation looks bleak, your enemies are laughing, and the hounds of hell are marching. But remember the Lord! Let's stand up for our families, our children, and our homes." As a result, the people went right back to the task, and Satan's plan failed.

Nehemiah said, "We're going to do it!" So they kept on building, and they finished the wall. Do not try to make yourself "feel" encouraged. You will never "feel" your way into a work, but you can work your way into a feeling. Just get yourself back to the job!

Get some rest. It may be as simple as that. Change your diet; get some exercise; resign from being the sovereign of the universe. Let God have His throne back. *He gives his beloved sleep* (Psalm 127:2). This deals with fatigue.

Then give yourself some think-time and say, "What am I doing? Am I doing a right thing the wrong way? Do I need to reorganize my life as I get these stones out of all of this rubbish that surrounds my life?"

Next fix your eyes on the Lord; remember God. You cannot look into the face of God and harbor fear in your heart at the same time. *For God has not given us a spirit of fear* (2 Timothy 1:7).

Finally, say, "By the grace of God, I will not give up, and I will not give in. God did not call me to fail." *Now thanks be to God who always leads us in triumph in Christ* (2 Corinthians 2:14).

5

THE WINNING PLAN
TO BREAK FINANCIAL BONDAGE

Every time God's people say, "Let us arise and build," the devil's crowd says, "Let us arise and blast." When God's people have a mind to work, the devil's crowd has a mind to wreck. The devil inspired certain philosophies and problems to keep Nehemiah, the leader and man of God, from leading his people—and to keep them from building the walls.

The devil will try everything he can to stop the person who strives to lead God's people forward to build with greatness for the glory of the Lord.

The devil will try everything he can to stop the person who strives to lead God's people forward to build with greatness for the glory of the Lord. The devil will first try derision. He tried to laugh Nehemiah's team out of their work for God. When that did not work, he tried discouragement. The devil tried to worry the people and weigh them down with the burdens of the project.

When the first two obstacles did not slow them down, he tried danger. Satan tried to cause fear by threatening them, but that did not work. However, he was not finished.

When all else fails, the devil comes to bring division. His purpose is to divide the people. This tactic took place during Nehemiah's rebuilding program. This division focused on money matters.

> *And there was a great outcry of the people and their wives against their Jewish brethren. For there were those who said, "We, our sons, and our daughters are many; therefore let us get grain, that we may eat and live." There were also some who said, "We have mortgaged our lands and vineyards and houses, that we might buy grain because of the famine." There were also those who said, "We have borrowed money for the king's tax on our lands and vineyards. Yet now our flesh is as the flesh of our brethren, our children as their children; and indeed we are forcing our sons and our daughters to be slaves, and some of our daughters have been brought into slavery. It is not in our power to redeem them, for other men have our lands and vineyards"* (Nehemiah 5:1-5).

The most sensitive nerve in the human body is the one that runs from the heart to the wallet. Evangelist Reinhardt Bonnke used to say to me, "God deserves all the credit, but He also appreciates cash in His work." If we are going to ultimately accomplish what our Lord has called us to do, then there will have to be enough money to get the job done. As visionary leaders, we constantly live with the tension between vision and provision.

In Nehemiah 5, there are two major sections regarding money and ministry — or finances and faith. These concepts impact all our lives. The first section relates to the problems of financial bondage, and the second section refers to the principles of financial freedom.

WE NEED TO REALIZE THE PROBLEMS OF FINANCIAL BONDAGE

The people in Nehemiah's time were under financial bondage. In Nehemiah 5:3, we read about strife and wages. The strife that was sown and the divisions that resulted were caused by problems involving wages, money, and finances.

In addition, the people were faced with a shortage of provisions to meet basic human needs and very high prices for those provisions. Nehemiah 5:2 talks about how difficult it was even to get the wheat and the corn that the people needed to eat.

When you read this passage, you will find that God does not want you to be the borrower; He wants you to be the lender. God does not want you to be the tail; He wants you to be the head.

The financial situation continued to worsen with the passing of time. People mortgaged their property. *There were also some who said, "We have mortgaged our lands and vineyards and houses, that we might buy grain because of the famine"* (Nehemiah 5:3). They did this to buy food. People are in deep financial bondage when they must mortgage their homes in order to feed their families.

As if all this were not bad enough, *there were also those who said, "We have borrowed money for the king's tax on our lands and vineyards* (Nehemiah 5:4). The people had gone to the finance company to borrow money to pay their taxes. High taxes are not something new; there have been high taxes around for a long time. However, when people must borrow money to pay the government what they owe, they are in serious bondage.

Financial bondage is not God's plan for His people. I encourage you to write down Deuteronomy 28:1-14. When you read this passage, you will find that God does not want you to be the borrower; He wants you to be the lender. God does not want you to be the tail; He wants you to be the head. God wants to bless His people above all the nations of the world and give them financial freedom. However, many people do not have financial freedom; they are in financial bondage instead.

As we move forward, let's ask our Lord for more than enough to do the work He has called us to do!

It is the devil's plan to keep God's people in financial bondage. Even though none of us are perfect in our handling of money, financial freedom will be the outcome when we begin to apply certain spiritual principles.

The devil wants to keep us in bondage and does not care what kind of bondage we are in as long as we are bound, but the Lord Jesus said He came to set us free: *Therefore if the Son makes you free, you shall be free indeed* (John 8:36).

When we talk to people about "handing me another brick" and "rebuilding the walls," there are some who will become frustrated with the vision. When we talk about doing something great and grand for God, their frustration over their own personal finances may cause them to turn on a brother or sister and criticize. This is the kind of division that took place when Nehemiah led his people to rebuild the walls. They were in a work, and the work was of God; it was God's plan—God's will.

However, there were some of the people who were under financial bondage which caused them to become irritated and frustrated, and they turned on one another—each to devour the other. It is the devil's way of dividing God's people—to keep them from doing the things God has called them to do.

We need to pray to the King of the universe for billions of dollars to be invested into the fulfillment of the Great Commission.

Financial bondage is not only for the poor, but it can also happen to the rich. *And I became very angry when I heard their outcry and these words. After serious thought, I rebuked the nobles and rulers, and said to them, "Each of you is exacting usury from his brother." So I called a great assembly against them. And I said to them, "According to our ability we have redeemed our Jewish brethren who were sold to the nations. Now indeed, will you even sell your brethren? Or should they be sold to us?" Then they were silenced and found nothing to say* (Nehemiah 5:6-8).

In Nehemiah's time, there was strife involving wages, a shortage of provisions to meet basic human needs, very high costs, the mortgaging of personal property, and borrowing to pay personal taxes. In addition to all this, the rich were squeezing the poor.

It was written in the Law of Moses that no Jew could charge interest to another Jew. He could charge interest to a Gentile but not to another Jew. However, many people were transgressing that law. They were squeezing the life out of their own people by charging exorbitant interest and putting their brethren under financial pressure and bondage.

When Nehemiah learned of this, he became very angry. He called them together, read the Word of God to them, and said, "Now, you quit this. You are being led by your greed." Those people who were wealthy and those who were taking financial advantage of the situation were just as much in financial bondage as those who were poor. Money is a wonderful servant but a poor master. There are people who have a lot of money who are still in financial bondage. The following four questions will help us to measure ourselves in this context:

1. **Do you have more faith in your money and your material goods than you have in God?** If so, you are in financial bondage of the worst kind no matter how rich you are. If you want to know how rich you really are, add up everything you have that money cannot buy and death cannot take away.

2. **Do you have ambitions that do not square with the will of God?** Are there things you want to do with your money — financial ambitions, financial goals — that are not in the will of God? If so, you are in financial bondage.

3. **Do you have a burning desire for money?** Do you have a burning desire for money or a desire to get rich quickly? If so, you are in financial bondage.

4. **Do you compromise your Christian ethics for the sake of money?** Do you compromise your Christian ethics and fail to honor moral obligations? If so, you are in financial bondage. Some people are very poor and in financial bondage. Some people are very rich but likewise in bondage. The devil has them.

We need to pray to the King of the universe for billions of dollars to be invested into the fulfillment of the Great Commission. If we are ever going to complete our God-given assignment, the kingdom of God will need more money than it has ever had in its history. As I write this, I do realize that a lot of money is spent in the Christian community that might be considered "wasteful" or short-sighted in the grand scheme of things.

One of the best ways for leaders to keep their teams together is to "become the illustration" — the God-given example of what it means to live out rock-solid principles before the team.

Along the journey to fulfilling the will of God in our lives, we will come upon huge challenges. Nehemiah discovered this. In the text we have been studying, Nehemiah is working hard not only to rebuild the walls but also to keep his team together until the job is done!

One of the best ways for leaders to keep their teams together is to "become the illustration" — the God-given example of what it means to live out rock-solid principles before the team. The greatest sermons we ever preach are those we illustrate by the lives we live every day.

In Nehemiah 5:14, Nehemiah is speaking against those who have been taking advantage of the poor. He begins with, *Moreover*; that is, "In distinction to this, in contrast to this, I want you to notice the way I live."

He was not the kind of a leader who says, "Don't do as I do; do as I say to do." He was the kind of a leader who could say with the Apostle Paul, *Be followers of me, even as I also am of Christ* (1 Corinthians 11:1). He could say with integrity, "Do as I do." "Moreover," Nehemiah says, "I'm going to tell you the way I live with my finances."

WE NEED TO REALIGN TO THE PRINCIPLES OF FINANCIAL FREEDOM

I want you to see how this great leader, this man of God, lived before his team. We have discussed previously the problems of financial bondage. Now we are going to share the principles of financial freedom.

Methods may come and go, but principles remain the same. The more effectively we can align ourselves with biblical principles, the more successful we will become over time. Everyone has the right to be financially free because the Bible says, *And my God shall supply all your need according to His riches in glory by Christ Jesus* (Philippians 4:19). We simply need to apply the financial principles God has set forth in His Word.

Value the Principle of Priority

There is the principle of priority: *Moreover, from the time that I was appointed to be their governor in the land of Judah, from the twentieth year until the thirty-second year of King Artaxerxes, twelve years, neither I nor my brothers ate the governor's provisions* (Nehemiah 5:14).

Nehemiah was saying, "I was the governor of this whole area, appointed by the king; and I had every right to tax the people. I had every right to have my needs supplied because I, as the governor, ought to draw a certain salary." Notice, however, what he says in verse 15: *But the former governors who were before me laid burdens on the people, and took from them bread and wine, besides forty shekels of silver. Yes, even their servants bore rule over the people, but I did not do so, because of the fear of God.*

Nehemiah was a remarkable man. He had certain rights and prerogatives but chose not to exert them. He said instead, "I refused to take what was rightfully mine because I feared God."

In other words, "We were in such a state of emergency and there was such turmoil that I was willing to forego my rights in order that God might be glorified." The bottom line was that Nehemiah chose to put God first. He had his priorities straight. Are you willing to do this? Are you willing to lay aside your financial rights and put God first?

Do you want financial freedom? *Seek first the kingdom of God and His righteousness, and all these things shall be added to you* (Matthew 6:33). As long as you put your business, your ministry, your plans, your desires, your ambitions, and your goals first, you will never know financial freedom.

The will of God meant more to him than anything else. If money is your god, if money is your goal, you will never know financial freedom.

On the other hand, if you get your priorities in order, if you will *seek first the kingdom of God and His righteousness*, then all the things you need *shall be added to you*. That is the promise of Jesus to us!

Nehemiah understood the principle of priority. He looked at the things he could have done — and done legally, within his rights — but he said, "I didn't do them because I want to glorify God." The will of God meant more to him than anything else. If money is your god, if money is your goal, you will never know financial freedom. Whether you are rich or poor, you will be in bondage.

If you do not put God first, you are foolish because you are playing a losing game. You may say, "Well, it's hard for me to trust; I deal in reality." Let me ask: What is true reality?

You may say, "My business is real; my house is real; my broken-down car is real." Yet I would contend that true reality is only found in those things that will last. *While we do not look at the things which are seen, but at the things which are not seen. For the things which are seen* are *temporary, but the things which are not seen* are *eternal* (2 Corinthians 4:18).

Reality is not in something you can see, taste, touch, smell, or feel. Reality is in God! If we are putting our trust in things that we can see, touch, taste, smell, feel, and count, we are living in a world of illusion. The things that are seen are temporal; the things that are not seen are eternal. We need to put the principle of priority into practice!

Voice the Principle of Productivity

I remember as if it were yesterday when I moved from Mobile, Alabama, to Springfield, Missouri, to attend Central Bible College. I had transferred to CBC as a second semester junior. After I had moved into the dorm, I became acquainted with my dorm mate.

One afternoon he and I were talking about being involved in ministry while attending Central Bible College. I told him, "I plan to be out speaking a lot while I attend CBC."

His response was, "You will not be able to speak a lot while you are here."

"Why not?" I asked.

"Because there are a lot of us who would like to have that opportunity, but we are unable to do so," he said. "There are just so many ministers and preachers who live in the Springfield area."

When I heard his response, I said, "Nevertheless, I plan to be traveling and speaking a lot while in college."

"Why do think you are the exception?"

I answered, "If you are willing to preach anywhere, there is a 'where' for you to preach."

I hope you grasped the lesson. If you are willing to serve anywhere, there is always a "where" — a place for you to serve.

As visionary leaders, we are going to have to work extremely hard if we are going to build something of significance. I know a lot of people who are coasting to the finish line of their lives. We need to remember: We can only coast downhill, not uphill. "Uphill" means climbing and extra energy.

If your goal is to get enough money in the bank so you will not have to work anymore, you may not understand what life is about.

Nehemiah goes on to say, *Indeed, I also continued the work on this wall* (5:16). Draw a circle around the word **work**: "I also continued the **work** on this wall."

If your goal is to get enough money in the bank so you will not have to work anymore, you may not understand what life is about. There are untold numbers of people who would like to have it arranged so they do not have to work anymore! The Bible says, *Six days you shall work* (Exodus 34:21). The same Bible that tells us to rest is also the Bible that tells us to work. Do you know why some people do not have financial freedom? It is because they think that **work** is a dirty word.

There are a lot of people who want a position but not a job. Nehemiah, who was financially well off, was the governor, and had a high-level government job, worked in the rubbish. He took his trowel and his sword and continued to build the wall! One of the main principles of financial freedom is spelled W-O-R-K! Why was Nehemiah such a free man financially? Priority — he put God first. Productivity — he knew what it was to go to work, and he was not afraid of work. He was not trying to get out of work.

View the Principle of Purity

The third principle is purity or integrity. Nehemiah stated: *Indeed, I also continued the work on this wall, and we did not buy any land* (5:16). What does this mean? He had integrity. This was a time of economic distress, and Nehemiah had a lot of cash. He could have gone in with his cash and bought this distressed property, but he refused to do it.

Just because it was legal did not mean it was right. Nehemiah refused to take advantage of someone else, and he refused to participate in a get-rich-quick scheme.

Proverbs 28:20 says, *A faithful man will abound with blessings, but he who hastens to be rich will not go unpunished.*

Nehemiah was a man who practiced purity and had integrity. Are you an honest person? Are you honest with God about your tithe? Are you honest with your income tax? Some say, "Honesty pays," but it may cost! Are you honest when it costs? Are you willing to walk circumspectly, to walk in purity and integrity? No wonder Nehemiah was such a man of God!

Nehemiah knew and lived by biblical principles, and prosperity followed him all the days of his life. Just as he followed the Lord in the ups and downs of his life, we are also challenged and commissioned to build our lives for years to come upon bedrock principles that are Christ-centered.

Our Lord has called and commissioned His servants to build and rebuild our lives and ministries for the glory of God. In the midst of this, there will be times when we have to get the rubbish out of the way so we can get to the building stones of goodness, greatness, and grandness. While we are in the process of moving from what does not matter to what truly matters, the enemy of our soul, the devil, will attack us to discourage us and distract us, to worry us and weigh us down. Yet we must continue to "pick up another brick" and just keep moving forward. There is no easy, quick way to get this done.

Our Lord has called and commissioned His servants to build and rebuild our lives and ministries for the glory of God.

Additionally, each of us are going to need the financial resources to complete the huge task our Lord has given us. Thus far in our Hand Me Another Brick series, we have learned the principles of priority, productivity, and purity.

Venture With the Principle of Provision

As we continue to move forward in the fulfillment of God's plan for our lives, we need to learn the principle of provision. *And at my table were one hundred and fifty Jews and rulers* (Nehemiah 5:17). Do you know how many Nehemiah had for dinner every night? 150! How would you like to have 150 for dinner every night for 12 years? Who paid the bill? The government? No, Nehemiah paid the bill. *And at my table were one hundred and fifty Jews and rulers, besides those who came to us from the nations around us* (Nehemiah 5:17).

In addition to the 150, the people were always bringing guests with them. What did they eat? *Now* that *which was prepared daily* was *one ox* and *six choice sheep. Also fowl were prepared for me, and once every ten days an abundance of all kinds of wine. Yet in spite of this I did not demand the governor's provisions, because the bondage was heavy on this people* (Nehemiah 5:18).

Wasn't Nehemiah an awesome leader? Nehemiah gave the best. He did not just give the people the old, cast-off things. He took the very best he had and set these people down—several hundred people a day. Nehemiah must have been a wealthy man! He fed them and fed them and fed them and refused to take the salary that could have been his as governor. Why? Because he had learned the principle that *it is more blessed to give than to receive* (Acts 20:35).

You say, "Where did he get all this stuff?" God kept giving it to him. Why did God keep giving it to him? Because he kept giving it away. He had learned simply to be a point of distribution. He had learned what Jesus taught: *Give, and it will be given to you: good measure, pressed down, shaken together, and running over will be put into your bosom* (Luke 6:38).

You cannot outgive God. Nehemiah found that out. Why did God take care of Nehemiah? Because Nehemiah put God first, because he walked in integrity, and because he was generous.

The Bible says very clearly that *he who sows sparingly will also reap sparingly*. You want a small crop? Just plant a few seeds. You want a big crop? *And he who sows bountifully will also reap bountifully* (2 Corinthians 9:6).

Validate the Principle of Prominence

The last principle is prominence. *Remember me, my God, for good,* according to *all that I have done for this people* (Nehemiah 5:19). Do you think God forgets when you are generous? He does not. Nehemiah depended upon God to reward him. He was not looking to a man; he was looking to God and depending upon God to supply his every need.

Nehemiah said, "Oh, God, now You think upon me. I have put You first; and now Lord, You are going to put me first." And God will do it. He will do it! As surely as there is a God in heaven, He will do it. You put God first, and God will think upon you for good and take care of you.

Let them shout for joy and be glad, who favor my righteous cause; and let them say continually, "Let the LORD be magnified, who has pleasure in the prosperity of His servant" (Psalm 35:27). Did you know that God enjoys our prospering? He really does. God does not want His people to be in financial bondage. He wants to set us free. The principles are priority, productivity, purity, provision, and prominence. We can trust God!

6

THE WINNING EDGE OVER EVIL INFLUENCES

We live in an era when millions of people make light of the supernatural, but heaven and hell are real locations. Our Lord Jesus Christ is the King of the universe while Satan is sailing a sinking ship on his way to an eternal hell.

The devil is not something to be laughed off, not something to be caricatured, and not something to be joked about. He is a decided fact, a destructive force but also a defeated foe. *Greater is he that is in you, than he that is in the world* (1 John 4:4).

The Book of Nehemiah is the story of the rebuilding of the walls around Jerusalem. The people of God saw a task that needed to be done and said, *We His servants will arise and build* (Nehemiah 2:20). The idea for the building of the walls of Jerusalem did not originate in the brain of Nehemiah but in the heart of God. Nehemiah and his massive team were simply thinking God's thoughts after Him.

This entire project was not Nehemiah's project but God's; therefore, Nehemiah could believe: *If God is for us, who* can be *against us?* (Romans 8:31). Consequently, he said, *The God of heaven Himself will prosper us; therefore we His servants will arise and build* (2:20).

However, every time the people of God say, *We His servants will arise and build,* the forces of the evil one say, "Let us arise and blast." When the people of God have a mind to work, the enemies of God have a mind to wreck. The first six chapters of the Book of Nehemiah tell of the devices of the devil — the things the devil did to try to stop the people of God.

The devil is not something to be laughed off, not something to be caricatured, and not something to be joked about.

If you want to know what the devil is going to do, find out what the devil has done. There is no need for a child of God who has a Bible to be ignorant of the devices of the devil. Paul said, *We are not ignorant of his devices* (2 Corinthians 2:11). I want us to see some of the poisoned arrows that the devil had already shot at Nehemiah, some of the tools that the devil had already used to wreck the work of God, and some of the dirty tricks that Satan had already pulled from his bag of evil.

In Nehemiah 4:1-3, we see that the first thing the devil tried was **derision**. He tried to laugh them out of a work for God. *Sanballat heard that we were rebuilding the wall, that he was furious and very indignant, and mocked the Jews* (v. 1). He tried by ridicule to drive them away from a work for God; but Nehemiah did not wither up or fold up because they laughed him to scorn. He realized that any true servant of God was going to be laughed at, and he determined that he would not be laughed away from a work for God.

When derision did not work, the enemy tried **discouragement**: *Then Judah said, "The strength of the laborers is failing, and* there is *so much rubbish that we are not able to* *build the wall"* (Nehemiah 4:10). When the job was halfway done, the people became discouraged. I know the devil would like to discourage me, and I know the devil would like to discourage you. It is okay to be weary in the work, but we must not get weary of the work. These people were just simply getting weary of the work. They were weighed down, they were wrought up, and they got discouraged. Then Nehemiah gave the battle cry, *Remember the* LORD (4.14).

When derision and discouragement did not work, the devil pulled out another arrow named **danger**. *And our adversaries said, "They will neither know nor see anything, till we come into their midst and kill them and cause the work to cease"* (Nehemiah 4:11). The devil threatened bodily harm! And he is not above threatening you with bodily harm if you take a stand for God. We must not think that the devil is soft. Jesus said the devil *was a murderer from the beginning* (John 8:44) However, Nehemiah was not going to be intimidated by the threat of physical, bodily harm. He put a trowel in one hand and a sword in the other and said, "Let us continue to build."

Nehemiah taught his people there are
no problems too big to solve—just people
too small to solve them.

The devil was not finished yet though. He tried **discord**. *And there was a great outcry of the people and their wives against their Jewish brethren* (Nehemiah 5:1). The devil said, "If I can't beat them any other way, I'll get them arguing among themselves. I'll spark discord — dissention in the ranks, and my motto will be 'divide and conquer.'" Nehemiah taught his people there are no problems too big to solve—just people too small to solve them. He found out what the problem was that was causing the dissention. He faced it; he fought it; he solved it; and the work of the building of the walls went on.

The satanic tactic the devil tried next was **depletion**. He tried to take away their resources. *There were also some who said, "We have mortgaged our lands and vineyards and houses, that we might buy grain because of the famine"* (Nehemiah 5:3).

The devil got them in debt and they were facing financial bondage, but Nehemiah taught them the principles of financial freedom. It is not God's will for His people to be in financial bondage. Nehemiah refused to let finances stop the work of God. When the devil tries depletion, remember: God's treasuries are still full!

In 1927, Charles Lindbergh flew solo across the Atlantic Ocean in a small airplane, The Spirit of St. Louis. Lindbergh told the story afterwards about how, having just gotten started on his flight, he found himself flying in a dense fog over Newfoundland. There was a lot of moisture, and he only had a compass. He had none of the sophisticated instruments our pilots have today such as an altimeter to show him at what altitude he was flying; however, he knew the direction he was going.

As Lindberg was flying, he could see that condensation was beginning to freeze on the plane's wings. He knew the ice would build up and, sooner or later, his plane would sink into the sea unless he turned around and went back. Lindbergh thought to himself, "This great adventure is going to come to an untimely end. What shall I do?"

In a moment of inspiration, he pulled the stick back; and that small plane started to climb up and up and up for what seemed like an eternity. He kept climbing and climbing and climbing until he suddenly burst out into the dazzling sunlight. No more fog, no more moisture. He flew all the rest of the way in the sunlight. (*WE*, G.P. Putnam's Books, 1927)

We do not have to fly in the fog of life; we do not have to be blinded by the deceptions of the devil. When the enemy comes at you, trying to get you to fly lower and lower, ask the Lord to pull you higher and higher. When the enemy tells you that you will not make it to your final destination, begin to quote the promises of God and demand he leave you alone!

As Nehemiah continued to move forward in the rebuilding of the walls, the enemy kept attacking with all he could throw at him. Satan was determined to stop the work of God. In addition to all the enemy had already done, he now came with a new series of attacks.

WE WILL FIGHT DISTRACTION

The next attack the devil tried was **distraction**: *Now it happened when Sanballat, Tobiah, Geshem the Arab, and the rest of our enemies heard that I had rebuilt the wall, and* that *there were no breaks left in it (though at that time I had not hung the doors in the gates), that Sanballat and Geshem sent to me, saying, "Come, let us meet together among the villages in the plain of Ono." But they thought to do me harm. So I sent messengers to them, saying, "I am doing a great work, so that I cannot come down. Why should the work cease while I leave it and go down to you?" But they sent me this message four times, and I answered them in the same manner* (Nehemiah 6:1-4).

What was the enemy trying to do? If the devil cannot defeat us as a roaring lion, he will try to defeat us as an angel of light. Sanballat invited Nehemiah to a Camp David-type meeting in a beautiful verdant valley called the plain of Ono. He said, "Well now, Nehemiah, don't be so obdurate. Just come on out here to the valley and sit down, and we'll talk this thing over."

Nehemiah was a man of God. He was wise enough to know that while the world may sometimes pretend to be friendly towards the work of God, the motives and methods of the world never change. *They thought to do me harm* (Nehemiah 6:2). He was not fooled. Nehemiah knew there was mischief in the making.

One of the dangers of any work for God is when it becomes successful in the eyes of the world. When the world can no longer whip it, it then tries to join it.

One of the dangers of any work for God is when it becomes successful in the eyes of the world. When the world can no longer whip it, it then tries to join it. The world wants to get on the good side of the people of God when it looks like their work is going to be successful. At first, the world will try to stamp the work out; but if they cannot stamp it out, they will try to neutralize it by entangling alliances. They will try to distract from the main work to be accomplished.

The story is told of a big game hunter who was hunting for bear. He wanted a bear because he wanted a bearskin fur coat. Finally, he saw his bear. As he took aim and prepared to squeeze the trigger, the bear said, "Now, hold on! Wait a minute! There's no need for you to shoot me. Let's go out here in the middle of the road, sit down, and talk this thing over. Be reasonable. After all, all you want is a fur coat, and all I want is a good meal." They met in the road and had a talk; and when it was over, the bear had a good meal and the man had a fur coat.

That is exactly what Sanballat was trying to do to Nehemiah. He said, "Come on now; let's sit down out here in the plain of Ono and talk this thing over," but Nehemiah would not be distracted. He said, "*I am doing a great work, so that I cannot come down* (Nehemiah 6:3).

The devil would love to get you distracted — to divert your church or ministry from the work you are doing. He knows that good can sometimes become the enemy of best. The devil would love to get a believer distracted and get them to step down from their God-given work. For example, there are mothers who have been called to raise their family. What a grand and glorious opportunity it is to be a mother and to raise those children for the Lord! But now the world beckons and says, "Come on out here. You can be successful in the business world." And the woman steps down — not up. She leaves her baby and goes out into the world to be a success.

God has a plan for our life — something He wants us to do, and we had better not substitute the good for the best.

My heart goes out to any woman who must work to put bread on the table and a roof over the heads of her children. What a tragedy though when a mother chooses to leave her babies in the hands of someone else and leave the work to which God has called her! She ought to say, "I am doing a great work, and the devil is not going to distract me." As someone once said, "It used to be that children learned at their mother's knee. Now they learn at some other joint."

Sometimes I see church workers — deacons, Sunday school teachers, ensemble members — doing a great work because it is the work to which God has called them. Then the world comes along and beckons and gives them honor.

There is a fraternity, a club, or a civic organization that says, "We need you"; and those people are so foolish as to be flattered by this world. They leave the work to which God has called them for something that someone else could do.

God has a plan for our life—something He wants us to do, and we had better not substitute the good for the best. We must find out what God wants us to do and refuse to be distracted by the devil. As the Apostle Paul said, so we need to say: *This one thing I do* (Philippians 3:13). Know what it is that God wants you to do and do it—just do it.

Sometimes churches get distracted. Do you know what the job of your church or ministry is? It is not building buildings. It is not raising money. It is the Great Commission—to win this world to Jesus Christ, to preach the gospel. It is amazing how many churches have put aside the task of evangelizing. Every now and then they think they might evangelize—like that is just something nice to do on occasion; but God has called us, and we dare not—must not—be distracted. We have a job to do; and by God's grace, we will do it.

The devil offered Nehemiah "the good" in place of "the best," and good things become bad things when they keep us from the best things. Nehemiah was invited to come to Ono for "a meeting of the minds," but he said no to Ono! He said, "I am doing a great work, and you are not going to sidetrack me."

When I was fifteen years old, I was the pitcher for our high school baseball team. I had been playing baseball since I was five. I grew up enjoying the sport.

After an afternoon of baseball practice, I was walking across an open field, knowing my mother would be waiting for me in her car on the other side to take me home. While I was walking, the Holy Spirit asked me, "What do you plan to do with the rest of your life?" I responded out loud while walking, "Lord, you know you have called me into the ministry. I will be a preacher all the days of my life."

The Holy Spirit responded to my answer with this question, "Then why are you spending so much time practicing a sport you will not be playing?" That was the last day I played baseball for our high school team. I had to make a decision.

Life is filled with practice, practice, and more practice. The key to success is to practice what you are called to do and to do it with all your might! Focus (or refocus) your energy all the days of your life on what really matters the most. If you sow early and long, your harvest in your later years will be greater than you could have ever imagined!

We learned in our last teaching that Nehemiah was attacked and invited to the "land of distraction." Satan will try to distract us in many different ways and on many different levels. However, to each distraction he sends, we must say, "I am doing such a great work, I don't have the time to waste on things outside of the will of God."

WE WILL FACE DEFAMATION

Then Sanballat sent his servant to me as before, the fifth time, with an open letter in his hand. In it was written: It is reported among the nations, and Geshem says, that you and the Jews plan to rebel; therefore, according to these rumors, you are rebuilding the wall, that you may be their king. And you have also appointed prophets to proclaim concerning you at Jerusalem, saying, "There is a king in Judah!" Now these matters will be reported to the king. So come, therefore, and let us consult together (Nehemiah 6:5-7).

Never underestimate the devil. Do you know what Sanballat was saying to Nehemiah? Nehemiah would not come down and have a little meeting with him, so Sanballat sent an open letter.

It was meant to embarrass Nehemiah; and this is what it said: "Nehemiah, it has been reported that you're trying to set yourself up as king. You're not really interested in these people. You're not really interested in rebuilding the walls. What you're doing, Nehemiah, is this: You're trying to feather your own nest. You're building a little kingdom for yourself. You intend to set yourself up as king." What Sanballat did was slander the motives of the man of God!

It is always true: When any church or ministry tries to do something for God, there are always those who say, "What about their motives?

It is always true: When any church or ministry tries to do something for God, there are always those who say, "What about their motives? Their motives are wrong." About any preacher who tries to lead his church in a great program, they'll say, "Well, he's trying to feather his own nest. He's trying to build a little kingdom for himself."

The devil is very clever, isn't he? And the devil knows how to use slander! What did Nehemiah do when they began to slander him and even wrote an open letter about it? He just kept on building the walls. I like that!

He said, "You're wrong. What you say is not true." He answered the charge clearly and plainly, and then he went on. *Then I sent to him, saying, "No such things as you say are being done, but you invent them in your own heart"* (Nehemiah 6:8). In other words, "They're lies, and I'm not going to run around trying to stamp out every lie."

Henry Ward Beecher once said, "Life would be a perpetual flea hunt if a man were obliged to run down all the innuendoes, inveracities, and insinuations, and misrepresentations which are uttered against him" (https://www.azquotes.com/quote). Nehemiah simply said, "I refuse to be on a flea hunt."

More than 150 years ago, Abraham Lincoln stated, "If I were to try to read, much less answer, all of the attacks made on me, this shop might as well be closed for any other business. I do the very best I know how, the very best I can, and I mean to keep on doing it until the end. If the end brings me out all right, what is said against me won't amount to anything. And if the end brings me out wrong, ten angels swearing that I was right would make no difference" (https://www.goodreads.com/quotes/155759-if-i-were-to-try-to-read-much-less-answer).

You need not be frightened by slanderers. Anybody who serves God is going to be slandered. The servant is not better than his master (Matthew 10:24). Remember what they said about Jesus? That He was a winebibber and a glutton and in league with the devil himself. If you live for God in your ministry, in your business, in your school—wherever you are, you might as well get ready for detractors to impugn your motives. Do not get sidetracked! Just stay on the wall and wear them out.

Henry Ward Beecher once said, "Life would be a perpetual flea hunt if a man were obliged to run down all the innuendoes, inveracities, and insinuations, and misrepresentations which are uttered against him."

Architect William Van Alen had a grand structure in mind when he set out to design a skyscraper that would help revitalize a tired section of Manhattan in the 1920s, but it was not until automobile tycoon Walter P. Chrysler stepped up as financier that the race was on to build the world's tallest building. Van Alen and Chrysler found themselves pitted against one of Van Alen's former partners who was in the process of constructing the Manhattan Bank Building (now the Trump Tower) with the aim of claiming the "world's tallest" title. However, Chrysler and Van Alen managed to hoodwink the competition — and the entire city of New York — to win the day.

At the heart of the skyscraper wars of the '20s and '30s was the bravado of the industrial age — the quest to be the first, the biggest, the smartest, the best. In communicating to Van Alen the scope of what he wanted for their project, Chrysler demanded nothing less than "a bold structure declaring the glories of the modern age." Another of Chrysler's demands was a top-floor office suite and exquisite apartments for himself.

To make it so, Chrysler financed the construction entirely with his own money, intent on making the building a legacy for his children to inherit. Van Alen and Chrysler set out to create a grand structure informed by French Art Deco — and the automobile. This included ornamentation on the exterior of the building fashioned after the hood ornament and radiator cap of the 1929 Chrysler Plymouth.

The year was 1929. On paper, the Manhattan Bank Building project at 40 Wall Street with its 60-foot spire looked to stand 85 feet taller than the Chrysler Building. The latter was expected to ring in at 925 feet. However, Chrysler and architect William Van Alen were determined to claim the tallest building title — so much so that they secretly constructed a spire for their own tower and kept it hidden until the last moment. The 186-foot steel structure was built inside the Chrysler Building in four sections and then hoisted in place atop the building and riveted together, all in a mere 90 minutes. From the ground to the top of its surprise peak, the final structure measured 1,046 feet, handily beating the Manhattan Bank Building.

Unfortunately, the victory was short-lived. The Empire State Building surpassed the Chrysler Building in height a mere 11 months later. However, the Chrysler Building is still, to this day, the tallest brick building in the world. Though it may not remain the tallest of skyscrapers, its classic mix of machine-age aesthetic with jazz-age poetry makes it arguably one of the most beautiful and well-respected. In 2005, it was voted by 100 prominent New York architects, engineers, and critics as their favorite tower of all time.

It took more than 10 million bricks to construct the Chrysler Building! It took one brick at a time, squarely placed, to build a superstructure. So it is with our lives; we must learn to build our lives one brick at a time, against all odds, for the glory of God.

> *For they all* were trying to *make us afraid, saying, "Their hands will be weakened in the work, and it will not be done." Now therefore, O God, strengthen my hands. Afterward I came to the house of Shemaiah the son of Delaiah, the son of Mehetabel, who was a secret informer; and he said, "Let us meet together in the house of God, within the temple, and let us close the doors of the temple, for they are coming to kill you; indeed, at night they will come to kill you* (Nehemiah 6:9-10).

WE WILL FEEL DISMAY

The devil came to Nehemiah saying, "They're after you. Run for your life!" He tried to put dismay into the heart of the man of God. The devil is the sinister minister of fear; and if he cannot stop us by slander or distraction, he will try to fill our hearts with fear because fear weakens us. *For they all* were trying to *make us afraid, saying, "Their hands will be weakened"* (Nehemiah 6:9).

Fear will weaken a church; fear will weaken a preacher. It is hard to serve the Lord with the icy fingers of fear on you. Fear turns your blood to ice water. It weakens your knees and stops you from the work of God. Are you afraid? Are you afraid that the work might not prosper? Are you afraid of what the devil may do to you if you take a stand for God? Over 365 times — one time for every day in the year — God said, "Do not fear." Isaiah 41:10 tells us, *Fear not, for I am with you; Be not dismayed, for I am your God. I will strengthen you.*

We need men and women of God today who are not afraid of the devil and who refuse to be intimidated!

The devil loves to make us afraid; he loves to get people cowering, but this is what fear will do: Fear will degrade our Lord. Fear is an insult to God who said, *I am with you.* Fear will destroy your life. You will become like the man who jumped on a horse and rode off in all directions. You will not get anything done. Fear is infectious. It will disturb your friends and delight your foes. When your enemies see you afraid, it will nerve them; but when they see you full of courage, it will unnerve them. *Be strong and of good courage* (Joshua 1:9). We need men and women of God today who are not afraid of the devil and who refuse to be intimidated!

The devil has a special demon — a demon of fear. It does not come from God *for God has not given us a spirit of fear, but of power and of love and of a sound mind* (2 Timothy 1:7). Are you a worrywart? One lady said, "Don't tell me it does no good to worry; most of the things I worry about never come to pass." Oh, how the devil wants to make us worry and fill us with dismay!

Find out what God wants you to do;
and whatever God has called you to do,
do not let the devil intimidate you and keep
you from your God-given goal.

Find out what God wants you to do; and whatever God has called you to do, do not let the devil intimidate you and keep you from your God-given goal.

WE WILL FLEE DECEPTION

When the devil could not defeat Nehemiah with distraction, defamation, or dismay, he tried one more thing. He does not give up easily, does he? This time the devil tried deception. Perhaps this was the hardest thing of all for Nehemiah to spot.

In Nehemiah 6:10, we read, *Afterward I came to the house of Shemaiah the son of Delaiah, the son of Mehetabel, who was a secret informer; and he said, "Let us meet together in the house of God, within the temple, and let us close the doors of the temple, for they are coming to kill you."* Notice how Nehemiah responded: *I perceived that God had not sent him* — underscore that phrase, "I perceived" — *I perceived that God had not sent him at all, but that he pronounced* this *prophecy against me because Tobiah and Sanballat had hired him* (Nehemiah 6:12).

Shemaiah was not a true prophet of God; he only pretended to be prophesying for God...only pretended to be on Nehemiah's side saying, "Nehemiah, I love you so much. I'm so concerned about you that God has given me a message for you; and this is hot from Heaven: Flee into the temple, Nehemiah. Shut the doors. God wants to preserve your life, and He sent me to tell you this."

However, this message was not from God at all. Shemaiah was a hireling. Nehemiah said, *I perceived that God had not sent him.* Nehemiah was not going to be deceived by the devil. The Bible says, *do not believe every spirit, but test the spirits, whether they are of God* (1 John 4:1). There are a lot of people—perhaps some are in your life right now—who pretend to be speaking for God when they are not speaking for God. The devil has his deceivers all over the world today.

For such are false apostles, deceitful workers, trans-forming themselves into apostles of Christ—note the next two verses—*And no wonder! For Satan himself transforms himself into an angel of light. Therefore* it is *no great thing if his ministers also transform them-selves into ministers of righteousness, whose end will be according to their works* (2 Corinthians 11:13-15 Emphasis added).

Ministers of Satan who appear as ministers of righteousness. False apostles, deceitful workers. The Bible says that Nehemiah perceived that this man was not of God. How did he know?

First, what this man told Nehemiah did not square with the Word of God. Shemaiah said, "Go into the temple and shut the doors behind you, and you'll be safe there." Nehemiah said, "I'm not going to sin." This man was asking him to sin. How? Nehemiah was what we would call a layman, and that part of the temple was reserved for the priest only. Thankfully, Nehemiah knew the Word of God!

Second, not only was there the outward, objective evidence of the Word of God, but there was also something subjective within Nehemiah. The Bible says we have no need that anyone teach us: *You have an anointing from the Holy One"* (1 John 2:20). I know in my own life there is a little bell within me that jingles when I am hearing the Word of God, and there is something else that sounds when I do not. When we are walking close to the Lord, the Holy Spirit of God will help us to perceive whether an individual is or is not of God and whether their words are from God or another source.

How easy it is to be deceived if we are not walking in the light of God's Word! We must keep our knees on the floor and our faces in the Bible in these days in which we are living.

We do not have to stumble in the darkness; we can walk in light. We do not have to be deceived by the devil; we have the Word of God, *a light that shines in a dark place* (2 Peter 1:19), and the indwelling Holy Spirit.

Listen again to what the devil tried to do to derail Nehemiah and his team of workers. The devil tried derision; he tried discouragement; he tried danger; he tried discord; he tried depletion; he tried distraction; he tried defamation; he tried dismay, and he tried deception—but none of it worked!

> *So the wall was finished* — the devil was not able to stop the work — *And it happened, when all our enemies heard of it, and all the nations around us saw these things, that they were very disheartened in their own eyes; for they perceived that this work was done by our God* (Nehemiah 6:15-16 Emphasis added).

My prayer is that we will do things in such a way that people will say, "That was of God! They didn't do that by themselves." We need to do something so great, grand, and glorious that it cannot be explained by promotion or propaganda or personnel or psychology. It can only be explained by the power of God.

We must keep our knees on the floor
and our faces in the Bible in these days
in which we are living.

Are you hungry for the people of this world to see something that causes them to marvel, "What's happening there? It must be the work of God!" God is in business. The world is hungry to see something that cannot be explained by human power or effort. What is there about my life or your life that cannot be explained? What is there, in your heart and in your life, that cannot be explained apart from God?

These are days for us to be supernatural, not superficial. These are days for us to be walking in the power of the Holy Spirit. These are days for the men and women of God to get a message from God and say, "Let us arise and build; and all of the dirty tricks of hell will not stop us, so help us God." And one day, it will be done; and people will say, "We perceive that this is the work of God."

7

THE WINNING WORD
AT WATER GATE

In June 1972, five men led by E. Howard Hunt, a former CIA agent, broke into the offices of the Democratic National Committee. The DNC was housed in a Washington, D.C., office complex called The Watergate. This activity was code-named "the plumber's operation." Its director was G. Gordon Liddy, a former FBI agent. The break-in was authorized by H. R. Haldeman and John Ehrlichman, two of President Richard Nixon's top advisors.

An investigation followed led by Senator Sam Ervin from North Carolina. The relentless questioning by Mr. Ervin resulted in White House Counsel John W. Dean, III, pointing an accusing finger at the President of the United States. In August 1974, President Nixon resigned in disgrace under the threat of impeachment, and "Watergate" became a household word synonymous with scandal. America was disgraced and embarrassed before the world over a place called Watergate.

Nehemiah 8:1-17 talks about a place called the "Water Gate." It was at the Water Gate that Israel experienced national repentance and revival. Nehemiah and Ezra had just led the Israelites in rebuilding the ruined walls of Jerusalem. With the temple and the walls completed, these men were now more interested in what happened inside the temple than in the buildings themselves. They wanted more than just survival; they wanted revival!

With all the people gathered in the street in front of the Water Gate, Ezra, the priest, stood before the people with the Word of God in hand.

With all the people gathered in the street in front of the Water Gate, Ezra, the priest, stood before the people with the Word of God in hand. The Word was read from morning until afternoon. As a result of reading and heeding the Word, repentance came; and revival was the climax.

It is the anointed preaching of the Scriptures that steers the sinner to Christ and strengthens the saints in the church. There is a famine in the land for Bible preaching — preaching that convicts men and challenges minds; preaching that is biblical, sensible, practical, and livable; preaching that exposes sin, exhorts the saint, and exalts the Savior. Genuine repentance and revival will be routine when the church gets into the Word of God. The church needs a Bible-based, Christ-centered Water Gate experience. Notice the progressive impact the Word of God had upon Israel.

WE NEED A HUNGER FOR THE WORD
(Nehemiah 8:1)

In Nehemiah 8:1, we see Israel's hunger for the Word of God. There was an assembly to hear the Word. The Scripture states that the people gathered themselves together in one place. There is something special about God's people coming together to hear the Word proclaimed.

There was also an agreement to hear the Word. This massive crowd came together as "one man." A true hunger for the Word of God results in a united people desirous to do the will of God.

In addition, the people were asking to hear the Word. They asked Ezra to bring out the Law of Moses. They were desperate for the Word. Israel had gone from rebuilding the walls to requiring the Word. They came to realize that the Book was more important than the building, and the Word was more important than the walls. Israel clearly understood that revival was not found in manmade monuments but was fostered in a hunger for the Word of God.

The church is undernourished and unable
to resist temptation because the world is loved,
but the Word is left out!

How hungry are you for God's Word? Most Christians are very religious when it comes to eating three meals a day, seven days a week. It is difficult for them to conceive of going several days without food of any kind. Still, many go days, weeks, and months without a hunger for the Word of God. The church is undernourished and unable to resist temptation because the world is loved, but the Word is left out!

It has been the hunger for the things of God that has made America great. The pilgrims wrote in the Mayflower Compact that their purpose was "for the glory of God and the advancement of the Christian faith." When the pilgrims got off that ship at Plymouth Rock, they all knelt on the beach and prayed, placing a cross there. The first public building to be constructed in America was a church. The first public meeting conducted was a worship service.

It was a hunger for God's blessing that drove the Continental Congress to their knees following the speech by Benjamin Franklin when he declared "that God governs in the affairs of men. If a sparrow cannot fall to the ground without His notice, is it probable that an empire can rise without His aid? We have been assured in the sacred writings, 'except the Lord build the house, they labor in vain that build it.' I also believe that without His concurring we shall succeed in this political building no better than the builders of Babel" (Benjamin Franklin Speech, Constitutional Convention, Philadelphia, Pennsylvania, June 28, 1787). After this oratory, the Congress knelt and prayed fervently that God would guide them; and the Constitution became a reality. The Senate was required to open every day with prayer, and this nation was born of a hunger for the things of God.

It has been said that the tremendous economic difference between South America and North America is not due to the lack of natural resources but that men went to South America seeking gold while men came to North America seeking God. The church is in perilous need of a Water Gate revival, beginning with a hunger for the Word of God. Are you willing to go to the Water Gate?

WE NEED A HEARING OF THE WORD
(Nehemiah 8:2-3)

Throughout the Bible, the "gate" or "gates of the city" have authoritative significance. In Genesis 19, Lot sat at the gate of the city. He had gone from looking at the city to living in the city to helping lead the city. The gate was the place where the leaders would gather regarding the management and leadership of the city. It was a place of authority.

In the New Testament, Jesus said *the gates of Hades shall not prevail against it* [the Church] (Matthew 16:18 Emphasis added). In other words, the leaders of the demonic world will never be able to manage or overcome the Church. So often we forget the real battles of life are not physical but spiritual; they are not against flesh and blood but against principalities and powers of the unseen world.

If we will fill the pulpit, our Lord will fill the building. I believe church attendance is down in the West because preaching is down in the pulpit.

When Nehemiah and his massive team were rebuilding the walls, they would have come in contact with all twelve gates of the city. The gate we are focusing on is the Water Gate. For us in the West, "Watergate" represents scandal and lawbreaking; but in Nehemiah's day, it was at the Water Gate that spiritual renewal came to the nation of Israel.

How much of the Lord do you have in your life? You have as much of the Lord as you want. Your level of thirst will determine your level of satisfaction every time. Jesus said, *If anyone thirsts, let him come to Me and drink* (John 7:37). Jesus did not say, "If you are empty" but "If you are thirsty." There are a lot of Christian leaders who are empty but not thirsty.

In Nehemiah 8, the leaders and the people had become thirsty for the Word of God in their lives, city, and nation. When they began to rebuild the walls, they did not know what they were going to find. When they found the Word of God, they called for Ezra to read it. If we will fill the pulpit, our Lord will fill the building. I believe church attendance is down in the West because preaching is down in the pulpit.

The Bible is easily accessible in many regions of the world. As a result of the accessibility of the Word, we often take it for granted. How big is your Bible? If you removed the sections you do not read, how big would your Bible be? We should strive to read the Bible through each year, digesting the principles and practices made available to us.

The hearing of the Word incorporated an appraisal of the people. Ezra brought the law before those who could understand it (8:2). The preacher must carefully evaluate the audience and relate the message according to their maturity. If there is going to be an appreciation for Bible preaching, then it must be adapted to the listeners and applied to their lives.

The hearing of the Word involved attentiveness to the preacher. Ezra read the scriptures for hours, and the people listened carefully to each word (8:3). When the Word of God is being proclaimed, do we think about what is being said, or do we take for granted that the preacher has done his homework and his message is biblically sound? Backslidden Christians do not want to hear the Word because it often bores them. It is sad that Bible preaching is merely endured in many churches while the music, entertainment, and special presentations are in demand. If Water Gate revival is going to happen in the church, there must be a hunger for the Word, a hearing of the Word.

WE NEED AN HONORING OF THE WORD
(Nehemiah 8:5-6)

When Ezra opened the book in the sight of all the people, they stood up (8:5). There was a genuine reverence for the Word of God. The Holy Word became an honored Word. The center of attention was not the speaker but

Scripture. Christians need to remember that without the Word of God, there is no hope of heaven, no joy in Jesus, no grace from God, no salvation from the Savior, and no strength from the Spirit. We would be outcasts forever, wandering in a world filled with chaos, trying to satisfy our inner cravings to know God. When a spiritual Water Gate occurs in a church, there will be Bibles everywhere and an excitement about preaching and teaching with a reverence for the Word that will be evident as the Word is honored.

Regardless of what our role is in society or in the church, each of us has a biblical role in renewal and revival.

There was also a godly response to the Word of God. They shouted *Amen, Amen!* and *bowed their heads and worshiped the* LORD *with their faces to the ground* (8:6). Israel got excited when the Word was preached. Their excitement was not based upon a preacher's personality or charisma but upon hearing the Word! Pure Bible preaching takes the attention off the preacher and places it on the Lord. Israel worshipped the Lord, not Ezra, the priest. When the Word is preached, there should be a vocal response as well as a physical response.

Regardless of their age, people must be challenged to respond to what they have heard. The true Water Gate alter service brings the congregation into a fresh dimension of humble worship before God. When Water Gate revival occurs, there will be a hunger for the Word, a hearing of the Word, and an honoring of the Word.

I have noticed an alarming trend regarding the percentage of people who do not bring their Bibles to the local church service. When I am a guest speaker, I ask people to stand in honor of God's Word and notice that most of the people do not even have a Bible with them. I cannot prove this, but I have concluded that if they are not willing to bring their Bibles to church, they probably do not spend much time reading it at home.

Another conclusion I have drawn when people do not bring their Bibles to church is that the preacher may not be faithfully preaching from it. Particularly in the West over the last 20 years, we have moved from preaching to presenting and from expounding to entertaining. I do believe that communication should be entertaining or attention-getting for the audience; but we have been drifting from the Word of God's being central to its being worked in.

What is amazing in Nehemiah's story is that he was not a person "called to handle the Word of God," yet Nehemiah knew what to do to lead the people back "to the law of God." Regardless of what our role is in society or in the church, each of us has a biblical role in renewal and revival. History is replete both with key preachers and key people serving in biblical roles for spiritual awakening. I encourage you to draw a circle, get inside the circle, and ask the Holy Spirit to renew you today. I believe spiritual awakening is the result of the spiritual leader's showing the population at large the way back to God.

If we are not careful as men and women of God, we can forget it is the "Holy Bible" for a reason. In other words, it is not just the "Bible" but the "Holy Bible." How we view Scripture will determine how we handle Scripture.

WE NEED A HANDLING OF THE WORD
(Nehemiah 8:7-9)

The Levites were determined to make sure that all the people comprehended what had been read. The large crowd was broken into smaller groups. The Levites read the Word of God distinctly and explained its meaning; they properly divided the Word of God. They did not twist, change, or abuse it; rather, they divided it correctly.

A person will desire to handle the Word after he learns to honor the Word. Some ministers have become so educated they no longer believe the Bible is the authoritative, inerrant Word of Almighty God. Not only does the church need old-fashioned Bible preaching but also old-fashioned Bible study.

Serious Bible study will be reflected in the pew when it is shared from the pulpit. The church does not need a spectacular personality to attract a crowd but a supernatural personality to attract a crowd and a supernatural power to confirm the Word. The church has had enough entertainment, storytelling, and joking from the pulpit. It is time for the church to dive deep into the Word of God and stay down long enough until she has gold nuggets in both hands that will change her for eternity.

When Water Gate revival happens, we will need the Word of God handled correctly. The people will not so much be interested in man's philosophies as in God's principles. Thus far, we have seen a hunger, a hearing, an honoring, and a handling of the Word.

WE NEED A HEEDING TO THE WORD
(Nehemiah 8:9-17)

Conviction was evident when the Word was heard (8:9). Israel began to weep in repentance. Individuals were confronted with their sin. Water Gate was the place where sin was purged when the Word was preached. It is this kind of sincere, straight, and scripturally sound sermon that is needed to bring conviction to our world today.

The preaching of God's Word not only brought conviction but also **consolation** (8:10), **calmness** (8:11), and **celebration** (8:12). When the hunger for God's Word has been restored and repentance has resulted, there will come forth a mighty wave of joy and celebration. Israel celebrated when the Word was made known to them.

The church today needs to hear and heed,
receive and respond, and listen
and live the Word of God.

Moreover, the heeding of the word meant **compliance** with the Word. Israel discovered a feast that had been neglected, the Feast of Booths (8:13-17). For seven days God's people complied with the Word and observed this feast. Israel obeyed the commandments of God. The church today needs to hear and heed, receive and respond, and listen and live the Word of God. Obedience to the Scripture reveals revival.

Almost two hundred years ago, Alexis de Tocqueville, a Frenchman, came to America to find out what made this country great. At the end of his search, he wrote these words: "I sought for the greatness and genius of America in her commodious harbors and her ample rivers — and it was not there . . . in her fertile fields and boundless forests and it was not there . . . in her rich mines and her vast world commerce — and it was not there . . . in her democratic Congress and her matchless Constitution — and it was not there. Not until I went into the churches of America and

hear her pulpits aflame with righteousness did I understand the secret of her genius and power. America is great
because she is good, and if America ever ceases to be good,
she will cease to be great" (*Democracy in America*, Penguin
Classics, 2003 [first published 1835]).

8

THE WINNING WORSHIP IN GOD'S HOUSE

We need to ask ourselves this question today: If every member of the church were just like us, what kind of a church would our church be?

If everybody sang as we sing in the song service, if everybody prayed as we pray in the invitation, if everybody were to give as we give during the offering, if everybody invited people as we invite people, if everybody studied their Bible as we study our Bible, if everybody witnessed as we witness, what kind of a church would our church be?

We are prone to look around and ask questions like, "What's wrong with the church? Why is there the lack of revival? What will it take for the church to regain the cutting edge in our society and world?" If we want to know what is wrong with the church, we need to go and look in the mirror.

For the children of Israel and the children of Levi shall bring the offering of the grain, of the new wine and the oil, to the storerooms where the articles of the sanctuary are, where *the priests who minister and the gatekeepers and the singers* are; *and we will not neglect the house of our God* (Nehemiah 10:39).

Jesus Christ loves the church. Jesus Christ died for the church. In the Old Testament, the house of God was the temple; in the New Testament, the house of God is the church — not the church building but the people. In the Old Testament, God had a temple for His people; in the New Testament, He has a people for His temple; and the people are called *the house of God* (1 Timothy 3:15). We are the household of God, and we will not forsake it.

If our professional life outpaces our private life, we will bring frustration to ourselves and to those around us. It is always the inside that determines the success on the outside.

We are coming to the end of the *The Winning Qualities of High Impact Leaders*. I hope you have enjoyed it half as much as I have enjoyed writing and preparing each lesson. The last major lesson is centered on the theme of "the winning worship in the house of God."

As leaders, it is important for us to arrange for times of personal examination. If our professional life outpaces our private life, we will bring frustration to ourselves and to those around us. It is always the inside that determines the success on the outside.

WE NEED PERSONAL EXAMINATION

Nehemiah 10:39 is the climatic verse. It has been building for some time, and Nehemiah finally brings the thought or theme to full maturity. It is in the chapter just prior, Nehemiah 9:1-3, that the people made a personal examination of their lives: *Now on the twenty-fourth day of this month the children of Israel were assembled with fasting, in sackcloth, and with dust on their heads. Then those of Israelite lineage separated themselves from all foreigners; and they stood and confessed their sins and the iniquities of their fathers. And they stood up in their place and read from the Book of the Law of the LORD their God for one-fourth of the day; and for another fourth they confessed and worshiped the LORD their God.*

Notice the elements of personal examination.

Humiliation

We need to begin with humiliation. The people of Nehemiah's day did it with fasting, with sackcloth, and with dirt upon their heads. In Old Testament times, people would take dust or dirt, throw it up in the air, and let it come down upon their heads. We do not follow this custom anymore, but the spirit of it is certainly something we ought to emulate.

We sit in church haughty, unbroken, unbent; yet it is a broken spirit, a broken and a contrite heart that moves the heart of God

Humiliation means getting low to the earth. Our very word humus means "dirt." They put dirt upon their heads to show how low they were, how humiliated they were before God. There is one thing wrong with many churches in America: We sit in church haughty, unbroken, unbent; yet it is *a broken spirit, a broken and a contrite heart* that moves the heart of God (Psalm 51:17).

Holiness

There was brokenness and humiliation, and there was holiness. *Those of Israelite lineage separated themselves from all foreigners* (Nehemiah 9:2). What does that mean? It means that the people got alone by themselves; they got quiet; they came out from the world. *Come out from among them and be separate, says the Lord* (2 Corinthians 6:17).

We do not hear much today about holiness. Everything is sort of muddy; it is not separated anymore. We have a "good Lord, a good devil, a take-it-or-leave-it" type of Christianity. It seems as though the church is becoming worldlier and the world is becoming churchier. If this happens much longer, we are going to find houses of God forsaken all over America. The people in Nehemiah's day separated themselves. They refused to be chloroformed by the spirit of the age.

Honesty

Not only was there humiliation and holiness, but there was also honesty. The people confessed their sins to the Lord. Notice, they confessed their sins; they did not compare their sins to other people. We should not look around and see what anyone else is doing. When will we realize that our measurement of success or approval is not based upon what others do or fail to do? Our measuring stick is the Word of God and the Son of God.

Consider Him who endured such hostility from sinners against Himself, lest you become weary and discouraged in your souls (Hebrews 12:3). The term for "consider Him" is a mathematical term. The writer of Hebrews is literally telling believers to make a list of all the things they are going through in their lives. Once they have made their list, they are to make a list of all the things that Jesus Christ went through regarding the cross. Once both lists have been created, they are to compare their list with Christ's list. Once they have measured their lives in comparison to the life of Christ (not the lives of others), they will be renewed in their minds.

Herein lies one of the major challenges for each of us: personal examination. I challenge you to spend some quality time in introspection, asking the Lord for keen insights into your personal spiritual life.

WE NEED PRIVATE EDIFICATION

What does it mean to forsake the house of God? The writer of Hebrews asks the question: *how shall we escape if we neglect so great a salvation?* (2:3). The key word is "neglect." It is the world that rejects Christ, but it is the Church that can neglect Him; and neglect is a serious indictment.

In my generation, I have seen a move away from finding out first what is on the church's calendar before planning the family calendar.

Forsaking the house of God is usually the result of a gradual walking away. In Hebrews 10:25, we are admonished not to forsake the assembling of ourselves together. In this context, the pressure was on, and persecution was rampant. Christians were forsaking the assemblies due to the threat on their lives; but even in the midst of this terrible circumstance, the writer of Hebrews told them, "Do not forsake the assembling." This is strong language, but the communication and conclusions are clear.

In my generation, I have seen a move away from finding out first what is on the church's calendar before planning the family calendar. Today, many plan the family calendar first and then work in the church's calendar if it is convenient or profitable to them. Along with this paradigm shift, Christ, the head of the Church, has also moved down the totem pole of priority; however, there is no way to neglect or reject "the bride" without neglecting or rejecting "the groom at the same time."

As fellow leaders, all of us have a duty to our church, to the house of our God. It begins with our personal examination. Here is the question that all leaders must ask themselves: If every member of my church were just like me, what kind of church would it be? Next we need a private edification. Where is one of the greatest places to be edified? In the house of God!

Assemble Our Church

It is our duty to attend our church. Radio and television were never meant to be a substitute for church attendance. We use radio and television as an outreach to those who are not saved and as a help to those who are sick, shut-in, or unable to come for providential reasons—but never as a substitute for attendance in the house of God.

The Bible says clearly and plainly without a shadow of any doubt that we are to attend the house of God and are not to forsake *the assembling of ourselves together, as is the manner of some, but exhorting* one another, *and so much the more as you see the Day approaching* (Hebrews 10:25). The closer we get to the Second Coming of the Lord Jesus Christ, the more we ought to be in the house of God.

Some folks only come to the church three times—when they are hatched, when they are matched, and when they are dispatched—yet about belonging to the church. They do not belong to the church. They talk about the church belonging to them — the church does not belong to them. It is the Lord's church.

We are to be faithful in church attendance. Some say, "Well, I can get the message by CD or podcast; I can get the message by reading; I can get the message by radio or television." We do not go to church just to get a message! We go to church to meet with brothers and sisters in Christ.

I can see the noose as it is beginning to tighten. I can see the humanistic value systems of our world as they are plotting to destroy Bible-believing, noncompromising churches.

There is a sense in which the Lord is present when His people gather that we cannot experience in any other way. *For where two or three are gathered together in My name, I am there in the midst of them* (Matthew 18:20). There is no substitute for church attendance. It ought to be faithful; it ought to be regular. There is no one too bad to come and no one too good not to come. We all need to be in the house of God.

Assist Our Church

We also need to realize that it is not only our job to assemble in our church but also our job to assist our church. As the days get shorter, the churches of God in America are going to be under bombardment as never before. I can see the noose as it is beginning to tighten. I can see the humanistic value systems of our world as they are plotting to destroy Bible-believing, noncompromising churches. We are going to find ourselves a generation of twice-born people in a world of once-born people, and we

123

are going to be going against the tide. The church is going to come under attack. It is not only our job to attend our church but also our job to assist our church!

Advance Our Church

In addition, it is also our job to advance our church — to go out and bring others in. Jesus said, *Go out into the highways and hedges, and compel* them *to come in, that my house may be filled* (Luke 14:23). Have you ever won a soul to the Lord Jesus Christ? If not, why not? Do you invite people to church on Sunday; or do you just come in, sit down, and think you have done God Almighty a favor?

This is a day of good tidings! We sin against the Lord if we fail to invite people to the banquet, to the feast, to the fellowship that we have every Sunday. How can we say that it means more than anything else to us on the face of the earth and yet we do not invite others to come?

Applaud Our Church

We must attend our church; we must assist our church; we must advance our church; and we should applaud our church. We ought to love the Church. Let the criticism come from the devil's crowd, from those outside the Church. Do not criticize the Church. Love the Church. The Church is not perfect. As a matter of fact, it is a society of sinners who finally realized it. It is the only organization where you must profess to be bad before you can join — unless it is the Hell's Angels. You just say, "I am a sinner." That is the qualification for coming. It is a society of sinners who have realized they are sinners and have banded themselves together to do something about it. Selah! Think on these things!

Why do we love the Church? Because Jesus Christ loves the Church! *Christ also loved the church and gave Himself for her* (Ephesians 5:25). Not the buildings—the people! We, the Church, are the object of His love; and what He loves, we ought to love.

When Saul was on the road to Damascus, intent on persecuting the Church, Jesus arrested him on the road and appeared to him saying, *Saul, Saul, why are you persecuting Me?* (Acts 26:14). I can imagine Saul thought, "Whoever You are, I'm not persecuting You; I am persecuting the Church." But the inference is clear: When you persecute the Church, you persecute Jesus. When you forsake the Church, you forsake Jesus. When you honor the Church, you honor Jesus. The way you love the Church is the way you love Jesus for the Church is the body of Christ. He is the head.

Not only did Nehemiah and his people have a time of personal examination and private edification, but they also had a time of prayerful evaluation.

WE NEED PRAYERFUL EVALUATION

Then . . . stood on the stairs of the Levites and cried out with a loud voice to the LORD their God. And the Levites . . . said:

> *Stand up* and *bless the LORD your God*
> *Forever and ever!*
> *Blessed be Your glorious name,*
> *Which is exalted above all blessing and praise!*
> *You alone are the LORD;*
> *You have made heaven,*
> *The heaven of heavens, with all their host,*
> *The earth and everything on it,*
> *The seas and all that is in them,*
> *And You preserve them all.*
> *The host of heaven worships You.*

(Nehemiah 9:4-6)

The longest prayer in the Bible is found in Nehemiah Chapter 9. Verses 4-6 are simply the preamble. In Nehemiah 9, the people began to contemplate the blessings of God; they looked back at the past.

If the house of God is not going to be forsaken, there must not only be personal examination but also prayerful contemplation.

It is marvelous the way they evaluated God's great blessings upon them! In verses 19-31, they spoke of the provisions of God; in verses 22-23, they spoke of the promises of God; in verses 24-25, they spoke of the power of God; in verses 26-28, they spoke of the patience of God; in verses 29-30, they spoke of the punishments of God. As they reviewed the past, they talked about God's blessings and their failures. They looked backward and said, "Oh, how good God has been! But how we fail the Lord!"

If the house of God is not going to be forsaken, there must not only be personal examination but also prayerful contemplation. Think of the blessings of God. Think how good God has been to your church. Think how many homes have been put back together. Think how many teenagers have been rescued from sin. Think how many blessings have come to elderly people. Think how many people have been snatched from the jaws of hell and made citizens of heaven.

How I praise the Lord for His goodness toward His people! How I thank God for His provisions! How I thank God for His promises! How I thank God for His power! How I thank God for His patience!

Think on these things. How good God has been to you? After such evaluation, how can we ever doubt God's plan for our lives!

When we forsake the house of God or when the house of God is no longer part of the family's life and calendar, the outcomes are usually quite disappointing and even disastrous. I realize there are exceptions; but typically, a person gradually slip-slides away and then fully forsakes the house of God.

We have considered the importance of a personal examination, private edification, and prayerful evaluation; but if we are going to cross the finish line with great success, we will also need a purposeful engagement or determination to stay in the house of God. Why do we love the Church? Because Jesus Christ loves the Church! *Christ also loved the church and gave Himself for her* (Ephesians 5:25). Not the buildings—the people! We, the Church, are the object of His love; and what He loves, we ought to love.

When we forsake the house of God or when the house of God is no longer part of the family's life and calendar, the outcomes are usually quite disappointing and even disastrous.

We end our study of Nehemiah with this thought: The ultimate key to opening the door of God's great blessings is a purposeful engagement or determination.

WE NEED A PURPOSEFUL ENGAGEMENT

After Nehemiah and the people had prayed and contemplated the goodness of God, after they had examined their own lives and their own failures, and after they

127

had reminded themselves of the goodness and the greatness of God, they made a solemn, holy vow and a covenant before God.

Includes Covenant

And because of all this — that is, because of all of
the blessings of God — *we make a sure covenant and
write it; our leaders, our Levites, and our priests seal it*
(Nehemiah 9:38 Emphasis added).

*Now the rest of the people — the priests, the Levites, the
gatekeepers, the singers, the Nethinim, and all those who
had separated themselves from the peoples of the lands to
the Law of God, their wives, their sons, and their daughters, everyone who had knowledge and understanding*
(Nehemiah 10:28).

Involves Commitments

Some people say, "I don't believe in making a pledge.
I don't believe in signing a commitment." I want to thank
God that I have a book full of God's pledges and commitments to us! *For all the promises of God in Him* are *Yes, and
in Him Amen, to the glory of God through us* (2 Corinthians
1:20). As these people in the Bible saw what God had
done for them and thought about the blessings of God,
they made a covenant. They signed it, sealed it, and said,
"There are three things we're going to do." We must also
commit to do these same three things if we want to ensure
that the house of God is not forsaken.

Commitment to Faithfulness

The people first made a determination concerning their faithfulness. *These joined with their brethren, their nobles, and entered into a curse and an oath to walk in God's Law, which was given by Moses the servant of God, and to observe and do all the commandments of the LORD our Lord, and His ordinances and His statutes* (Nehemiah 10:29).

In other words, they said, "We are going to live by the Word of God. We enter into a covenant — we into an oath that we are going to be subject to the Holy Scriptures." Will you enter into that covenant? Will you live by His book? Whatever God says, will you do it?

Commitment to Their Families

They made a determination regarding their families, pledging that *we would not give our daughters as wives to the peoples of the land, nor take their daughters for our sons* (Nehemiah 10:30).

What did this mean? They were saying, "Our family life is going to glorify God. We are not going to lose our children to the world. We are not going to allow our children marry unsaved people." The Bible says, *Do not be unequally yoked together with unbelievers* (2 Corinthians 6:14). We must commit to bringing up our children in the fear and the nurture and the admonition of Almighty God (Ephesians 6:4).

Commitment to Their Finances

The people made a solemn declaration concerning their faithfulness that they would live by the Word of God and concerning their families that the devil will not get their children. They also made a declaration concerning their finances. *If the peoples of the land brought wares or any grain to sell on the Sabbath day, we would not buy it from them on the Sabbath, or on a holy day* (Nehemiah 10:31).

The people made a solemn declaration concerning their faithfulness that they would live by the Word of God and concerning their families that the devil will not get their children.

In other words, they said, "We are not going to transgress God's laws in business." Obviously, we are talking about people in the Old Testament—Jews who lived by the Old Testament laws regarding the Sabbath which was Saturday; but what does this mean to us as Christians today? It means that in our business transactions, our money is going to be rightfully gained and also rightfully given.

Also we made ordinances for ourselves, to exact from ourselves yearly one-third of a shekel for the service of the house of our God (Nehemiah 10:32). That is, "We made a law for ourselves. We wrote it down. We made a solemn commitment. We made a pledge that we are going to bring of our substance and our finances to the house of the Lord."

Notice carefully Nehemiah 10:38-39: *And the priest, the descendant of Aaron, shall be with the Levites when the Levites receive tithes; and the Levites shall bring up a tenth of the tithes to the house of our God, to the rooms of the storehouse. For the children of Israel and the children of Levi shall bring the offering of the grain, of the new wine and the oil, to the storerooms where the articles of the sanctuary* are, where *the priests who minister and the gatekeepers and the singers* are; *and we will not neglect the house of our God.*

These people had enough understanding to know that it takes money to carry on God's work. Do not get so heavenly-minded that you are no earthly good saying, "Oh well, I'm just interested in spiritual things. I'm not interested in material things." Jesus Christ had more to say about a man's relationship to his material goods than He had to say about heaven or hell. Jesus said, *For where your treasure is, there your heart will be also* (Matthew 6:21).

When we bring God's tithe to God's house on God's day and our love offering on top of that, we are making certain that the church, the house of God, will not be forsaken.

When we bring God's tithe to God's house on God's day and our love offering on top of that, we are making certain that the church, the house of God, will not be forsaken.

Here comes the climax to all of this: The people said, *And we will not neglect the house of our God* (Nehemiah 10:39).

I want to plead with you; I want to pray for you; I want to persuade you, my fellow servants in Jesus Christ, that you take these four powerful steps in the days ahead:

1. Make a personal examination. What kind of person are you? Do not look around and see what others are doing — examine yourself!
2. Make a private evaluation.
3. Make a prayerful evaluation. Look to see how good God has been!
4. Make a purposeful engagement. Declare to God and to your family, "We will not...we will not forsake the house of our God."

AFTERWORD

Our mindset will be the ultimate deciding factor between winning and losing in life. Please note that I did not say "winning or losing in a competition" but in life. Mindset is everything. I hope you will engrave this into your brain, mind, and soul. Our mindset should be considered the intangible X-factor that will strongly determine our future success in life.

We go in the direction of our most dominant thought. "As he thinks in his heart, so is he" (Proverbs 23:7 NASB). Our perceived reality will become the end product of our mindset. Our mindset is the true mirror reflection of who we truly are as a person. In other words, our mental outlook reflects the personal qualities we possess. On the one hand, if we expect to "just get by" or "to lose," the odds are that this will be our outcome. On the other hand, if we expect to succeed, we will need to step up in the game of life and give our best each day.

In *The Winning Qualities of High Impact Leaders*, Dr. James O. Davis not only gives us the mental map for our future success but also the motivation to apply this new map throughout the rest of lives. I have heard him say quite often, "Old maps will not work in new land." We must obtain new mental maps in order to navigate in unfamiliar territories. This dynamic resource will help to provide such a mental success map!

What Dr. Davis has learned from the motivation required to build the Global Church Network

(GlobalChurchNetwork.tv), the largest pastors' network in the world, he is now passing on to us. In one truly memorable scene in the film "Rocky II," Duke, the trainer of Rocky's opponent, Apollo Creed, tells Apollo why he should not fight Rocky again:

> *He's all wrong for us, baby. I saw you beat that man like I never saw no man get beat before, and the man kept coming after you. Now we don't need that kinda man in our life.*

The size of the person is determined by whatever it takes to stop them. There are times that a high impact leader is like a locomotive plowing through a solid concrete wall. They just keep on going.

This is not a book about influence but impact. What is the difference between influence and impact? If a friend goes fishing in the morning and comes back to the office in the afternoon, you will undoubtedly ask, "How did it go?"

---

*Dr. James O. Davis not only gives us
the mental map for our future success but also
the motivation to apply this new map
throughout the rest of lives.*

If your friend answers, "I influenced a lot of them," that is not the answer you are looking for. You want to know if they caught anything. That is the difference between influence and impact. A high impact leader has something to show for their influence. As you read this powerful resource, you will learn the eight overarching winning qualities of high impact leaders who have some-thing to show for their energy.

Both secular and sacred communities admire Nehemiah's leadership regarding the rebuilding of the walls of Jerusalem in 445 BC. When people stand in front of the "Wailing Wall" in Jerusalem, they are standing in front of the actual wall that Nehemiah rebuilt! Against all odds and opposition, he was able to reignite the vision, rally his team, and rebuild the walls in less than two months! Dr. Davis has utilized the dynamic leadership qualities of Nehemiah to write *The Winning Qualities of High Impact Leaders*. However, this book is far more than an exposition of the Book of Nehemiah. He draws *from* the deep well of Nehemiah's incredible life, work, wisdom, wealth, and worship for success.

Whether you are so discouraged and feel so small to the point that you could sit on the curb and dangle your feet from it or feel beaten up by the ridicule and harassment of others, Dr. Davis has brought to life, a winning strategy to help you to cross the seemingly vast divide between your failure and success.

Whether you are so discouraged and feel so small to the point that you could sit on the curb and dangle your feet from it or feel beaten up by the ridicule and harassment of others, Dr. Davis has brought to life, a winning strategy to help you to cross the seemingly vast divide between your failure and success. Just as Nehemiah was called to rebuild the walls of Jerusalem to help the Jewish people to fulfill their God-given, divine destiny, we are called to live a wide enough life to impact the people around us, lifting them to new heights!

As you read *The Winning Qualities of High Impact Leaders*, approach it with humility of spirit. Humility is about remaining hungry to keep improving and moving toward your success goal. A humble person does not under or overestimate their abilities. In addition, you will discover the balance between having a confident mindset yet a realistic view of your strengths and weaknesses to build the important walls of your life.

If you let it, this resource can help you evaluate your life both biblically and spiritually, turning you from a thermometer that reflects the temperature around you to a thermostat that regulates the temperature around you.

On the heels of humility is vulnerability. We must recognize the need to change and evolve as we age or as our goals broaden. We need to be willing to seek help in order to get the best out of ourselves. This book is not another self-help book or just another leadership book printed for the marketplace. Dr. Davis has masterfully combined the "inspiration" from God's Word with "information" for today's world. You are not just getting another person's point of view on high impact leadership but a true, biblical, step-by-step process of success. Just as Nehemiah and his team had to work super hard, exposing your humility and vulnerability will ensure you never get overly confident; and it will always remind you of where you came from and how hard you had to work to get where you are.

How many times have you competed in an event and wished you had done more training? Or finished an event and wished you had pushed yourself harder? Or stepped out into a new, huge project and wished you had prepared more and given more energy to its fulfillment?

As you read *The Winning Qualities of High Impact Leaders,* you are learning from a servant leader who has "been there–done that" and can testify to the fact of what it takes to rebuild a vision that others willfully tore down. Dr. Davis will lead you through the "rubbish of your night" like Nehemiah did 2,500 years ago and through the noise of ridicule and negativism, like Sanballat did to Nehemiah, until you are standing on the top of your God-given walls!

My sincere prayer is that as you read this timely book, you will be revived in your spirit and stirred deep within your soul. When the walls of Jerusalem were rebuilt, a revival for God's Word began at the Water Gate. Not only was Nehemiah never the same, but the Jewish people also turned back to the Lord. If you let it, this resource can help you evaluate your life both biblically and spiritually, turning you from a thermometer that reflects the temperature around you to a thermostat that regulates the temperature around you.

Just like life, game days are not infinite; and they are certainly not warm-ups. I believe this book will help you to make every day matter and every opportunity count!

Dr. Timothy Hill
Overseer of Church of God
Cleveland, TN

November 2019

CONCLUSION

Over the last 40 years, I have been fortunate to minister to and challenge leaders in more than 130 nations. I have invited them to be second-mile, visionary leaders where it is legal and illegal in every world region. With this in mind, I write to extend to you a personal invitation to develop the winning qualities of high impact leaders in your life!

> *Therefore we also, since we are surrounded by so great a cloud of witnesses, let us lay aside every weight, and the sin which so easily ensnares* us, *and let us run with endurance the race that is set before us, looking unto Jesus, the author and finisher of* our *faith, who for the joy that was set before Him endured the cross, despising the shame, and has sat down at the right hand of the throne of God* (Hebrews 12:1-3).

Our Lord has invited us to the **contest**. God has a race for YOU! Say it to yourself, "GOD HAS A RACE FOR ME!" The idea is that all of us, every one of us, is in the stadium of life. The stadium is packed and jammed with people from all over the world. Just as the emperor was looking down at those runners so long ago, our Lord from heaven is watching us as we run our race.

In the spiritual realm, we are runners and there is a goal for each of us. We are not running against one another. As far as one another is concerned, we are not in competition with each other.What are we racing for? We are racing against sin, against self, and against life itself to win the eternal prize. Our goal is not heaven. We are not running to try to qualify for heaven. Salvation is not a reward at the end of the race. Salvation is what puts you in the race in the first place. Salvation is not a reward for the righteous but a gift for the guilty.

The word for race in Greek is "agon." *Agon* is the word for "agony" today. The Hebrew writer is writing about a marathon. He is talking about a race that is grueling and agonizing. God has a race for you to run in your life.

In addition to the contest, we need to see the **crowds.** There are those in the grandstand to cheer us on in our race. In Hebrews 11, we read about all of the heroes of the faith — a gallery of the great. It is a picture of the saints in heaven. They are called *so great a cloud of witnesses* (Hebrews 12:1). I am not sure if the saints in heaven are watching us; however, we do know that our Lord is watching us.

These heroes of the faith inspire us to run our best. All of us need examples of excellence to challenge us to run better than we have ever done in our life. The life of Nehemiah persuades us to step out into the will of God — even though it will be difficult — and to believe that He will provide the path of success for us! Even though Nehemiah is not mentioned in Hebrews 11, his legacy of leadership challenges us to rebuild the walls of our life for the glory of God.

Conditioning is required to develop the winning qualities of high impact leaders. *Therefore we also, since we are surrounded by so great a cloud of witnesses, let us lay aside every weight, and the sin which so easily ensnares us, and let us run with endurance the race that is set before us* (Hebrews 12:1).

When we are running a race, we cannot allow anything to slow us down. There must be discipline if we are going to run to win. He mentions two aspects of this discipline: the weights that slow us down and the sins that trip us up.

We are to lay aside every weight. *Onkos* is the Greek word for "weight." There are things in life that are not necessarily wrong; but if they slow us down in the race before us, we need to lay them aside. There is nothing wrong with an overcoat, but it will slow us down in the race. There is nothing wrong with cowboy boots but wearing them in the race will slow us down.

What do runners do when they run? They strip down to the bare necessities. Here is the point: Good things are bad things if the good things keep us from the best things. There are a lot of things that are not necessarily wrong, but they are wrong for us if they slow us down.

All things are lawful for me, but all things are not expedient (1 Corinthians 6:12 KJV). When we think of expedient, we think of an expedition. An expedition is something that is going somewhere. Paul is saying that if this thing does not help us get to the place we are supposed to go, for us it is wrong.

I fly hundreds of flights each year. I have not checked a single piece of luggage since 2002. Why? I cannot afford the time to chase lost bags or stand at the baggage carousel approximately 6 hours a month or 72 hours a year or 700 hours in a decade!

I do not have time to read good books because I have not read the best ones. Now a good book may be a recreational book because God wants you to have recreation, but so many times we are just simply wasting time. We lay aside every weight that slows us down.

Would you think about some things in your life right now? What is there in your life that if you eliminated, you could run the race better? What are you spending time on? What are you spending money on? What are you spending thoughts on? What are you spending energy on? If you eliminated those things, you could get down the track faster. Life would be simpler if it were a choice between good and bad; but it is not. It is a choice between good and best and sometimes between best and best.

Then there are the sins that must be laid aside: *the sin which doth so easily beset us* (Hebrews 12:1 KJV). The Greek word means "to entangle" — to trip us up. We must deal with sin as sin will deal with us.

Pet sins are no friend. We need to treat sin as it will treat us. Be ruthless with your sin. RUTHLESS! Have no mercy on that sin. None! Sin will have no mercy on you. It will entangle you and you will fall, and you will fail to win the prize.

Moreover, each of us has a **course**, the race that is set before us (Hebrews 12:1 KJV). What is your course? What is the race that God has marked out for you?

Has God called you to run the race on the music track? Has the Lord directed to the medical field for His glory? Have you been called to be a homemaker? Then get on the track and run your best. God has set a race before us. My race is not your race; we run the course that is set before us.

I become weary of watching Christian leaders race against each other. We are not even on the same track. We are not racing against each other but against Father Time. The greatest tragedy would be for our life to come to a close and our race not be finished.

If we are going to have the qualities of winning leadership, we must have **continuance**. We are to "run with patience" or "endurance." We are to bear up under the pressure and keep running.

We may leave a song unfinished, a sermon undone, a house unbuilt, a flower unplanted, needlework undone, or a book unread; but when it comes to running "the race" that is "marked out for us," we are called to finish it before our homegoing takes place. Run with patience! Don't quit! Don't quit! Don't quit!

If we are going to possess the winning qualities of high impact leaders, we will need the best possible **coach**. *Looking unto Jesus, the author and finisher of* our *faith* (Hebrews 12:2).

Why do you look unto Jesus? He is the author of our faith. The word "author" actually means "example." Faith comes by beholding Jesus Christ. If you are having difficulty with your faith, it is because you have not really seen Jesus.

The word "finisher" means the "perfecter" and the "completer." It means He is the one who gives you the strength for the race. HE is the finisher. If you know Him, you are going to finish.

Looking UNTO Jesus. Our text does not say "looking at Jesus" but *looking unto Jesus*. What is the difference? Imagine that you have debts you cannot pay, but you have a friend who says, "look to me." They are not saying look at me but look to me. "Depend upon me. I will see you through. I will take care of you." It is faith in Jesus, not facts about Jesus. It is looking unto Jesus, not looking at Jesus, that gives the strength to run the race.

We are to look away from everything else and put our eyes completely on our example, Jesus Christ. We are not look at other things. We are not to put our eyes on Satan; he will terrify us or entice us. We are not to put our eyes upon the sins of those for whom Jesus died. We must get our eyes off hypocrites and look to the Lord Jesus Christ. We are not to put our eyes upon ourselves.

The devil is diabolical and deceptive. He will try to get us to look at anything or anyone other than Jesus. He will try to get us to examine our faith and wonder if it is strong enough to run the race. Look to Jesus! Look away from everything else and look to the Lord Jesus Christ. He is the coach. The Lord Jesus is the author of our faith. The Lord Jesus is the finisher of our faith.

Last, when we run our God-given race to win, we will receive a **crown.** *Looking unto Jesus, the author and finisher of our faith, who for the joy that was set before Him endured the cross* (Hebrews 12:2). There was a crown for the Lord Jesus. Do you know what His crown was? You and I! We are the prize that He ran all the way to the cross for. At the end, he said, *It is finished!* (John 19:30).

Each of us who finish the race the Lord has given to us will receive a crown. Two thousand years ago when an athlete would win in the Olympic games, his name would be proclaimed throughout the whole country. There would be a parade in his honor. They would scatter flowers across his pathway. The runner would be presented with costly gifts. Sculptors would sculpt statues of the runners who won the race.

Every runner who wins receives a prize. Are you running to win an eternal prize? I am. I hope you are. The Bible says we are to run that we might win. *For what is our hope, or joy, or crown of rejoicing? Is it not even you in the presence of our Lord Jesus Christ at His coming?* (1 Thessalonians 2:19).

Are you in the race God has marked out for you? If not, get in the race today. You have been given the opportunity to possess the winning qualities of high impact leaders and to run the greatest race of your lifetime upon this earth. It would be most tragic for your life to end and your race not to be finished.

ABOUT THE AUTHOR
AND HIS RESOURCES

Dr. **James O. Davis** is the founder of Cutting Edge International and Global Church Network, a growing coalition of more than 2,600 Christian ministries and denominations synergizing their efforts to build a premier community of pastors worldwide to help plant five million new churches for a billion soul harvest and to mobilize the whole body of Christ toward the fulfillment of the Great Commission. With more than 650,000 churches, the Global Church Network has become the largest pastors' network in the world.

Christian leaders recognize Dr. Davis as one of the leading networkers in the Christian world. More than 80,000 pastors and leaders have attended his biennial pastors' conference and leadership summits across the United States and in all major world regions. Dr. Davis is considered to be in the *Top Ten Christian Influencers in the World.*

In October 2017, Dr. Davis spearheaded and hosted *The Wittenberg 2017 Congress* in Berlin, Germany. The Wittenberg 2017 Congress celebrated the 500th anniversary of Martin Luther's nailing his 95 Theses on Castle Church door in Wittenberg, Germany. This historic congress brought together more than 650 influential leaders from more than 80 different denominations and every world region.

Dr. Davis served 12 years leading 1,500 evangelists and training thousands of students for full-time evangelism as the National Evangelists' Representative at the National Office of the Assemblies of God. Ministering more than 45 weeks per year for 40 years, Dr. Davis has now traveled over 10 million miles to minister face-to-face to millions of people in more than 130 nations.

Dr. Davis earned a Doctor of Ministry in Preaching at Trinity Evangelical Divinity School and two master's degrees from the Assemblies of God Theological Seminary.

DR. JAMES O. DAVIS'S BOOKS AND RESOURCES

- *We Are The Church: The Untold Story of God's Global Awakening* (coauthored with Dr. Leonard Sweet)
- *The Forgotten Baptism: Your Visionary Path To Success* (coauthored with Dr. Kenneth Ulmer)
- *How to Make Your Net Work: Tying Relational Knots for Global Impact*
- *The Forgotten Baptism: Your Leadership Path to Fulfilling Your Vision* (coauthored with Dr. Kenneth Ulmer)
- *Scaling Your Everest: Lessons from Sir Edmund Hillary*
- *Gutenberg to Google: The Twenty Indispensable Laws of Communication*
- *The Great Commission Study Bible* (coauthored with Dr. Ben Lerner)
- *The Billion Soul Story*
- *12 Big Ideas*
- *The Pastor's Best Friend: The New Testament Evangelist*
- *Living Like Jesus*
- *The Preacher's Summit*
- *What to Do When the Lights Go Out*
- *It's a Miraculous Life!*
- *Signposts on the Road to Armageddon*
- *Beyond All Limits: The Synergistic Church for a Planet in Crisis* (coauthored with Dr. Bill Bright)
- *The Adrian Rogers Legacy Collection*
- *The Elmer Towns Legacy Collection*
- *The Stephen Olford Preaching Collection*

His quotes and articles have appeared in scores of magazines, newspapers, and blogs.

Dr. Davis resides in the Orlando area with his wife, Sheri, and daughters, Olivia and Priscilla. They have two children, Jennifer and James, who reside in heaven.